Destination Buchenwald

DESTINATION BUCHENWALD

COLIN BURGESS

Kangaroo Press

Also by Colin Burgess

The Diggers of Colditz (with Jack Champ)
Aircraft
Space: The New Frontier
Laughter in the Air (with Max Harris)
More Laughter in the Air
Pioneers of Flight
Prisoners of War
  (with Hugh Clarke & Russell Braddon)
Barbed Wire and Bamboo (with Hugh Clarke)
Freedom or Death
Oceans to Orbit

Cover Design by: **Darian Causby**

Background and bottom: Buchenwald as found by liberating Allied armies.
Centre right: Pilot Officer Bob Mills, post-Buchenwald.
Back cover: The Cremetoria. (Courtesy Imperial War Museum)

First published in 1995 by Kangaroo Press Pty Ltd
3 Whitehall Road Kenthurst NSW 2156 Australia
P.O. Box 6125 Dural Delivery Centre NSW 2158
Printed by Australian Print Group, Maryborough, Victoria 3465

ISBN 0 86417 733 X

This book is dedicated to the two airmen who
never left Buchenwald:

Flying Officer Philip Derek Hemmens, RAF
First Lieutenant Levitt Clinton Beck, Jr., USAAF

'Only those who have been prisoners have any
conception of the horrors of being a prisoner,
or of the ineffable joy of release; of the terrible
rise and fall of the spirit, the fluctuations
between the delirium of happiness and
madness of despair, attendant upon the
fluctuating hopes and fears as the possibility
of release advances and retreats.'

P.C. Wren, *Beggars' Horses*

CONTENTS

FOREWORD

It is difficult to comprehend the totality of the evil which existed in Buchenwald, just as it is beyond human understanding to grasp the meaning of 'The Absolute' or the ultimate and unknowable. It was an evil as black as night.

I am honoured to be asked to write a foreword to Colin Burgess' excellent and well-researched book which opens the gates on one of Hitler's most notorious concentration camps, and leaves us in no doubt about the brutality and bestiality which caused tens of thousands to suffer the torments of Hell. We can feel the blows of the SS, hear the stamping of jackboots and the screams of the prisoners resounding across the Appell Platz through lice-infested huts, the stinking aborts, the places of execution and the crematorium.

The Allied airmen who arrived in Buchenwald during that summer of 1944, when our armies were sweeping towards Paris, were all young men who had been on normal air operations; they had no expectation, if sanguine, of eventual survival; if unlucky they could expect 'the chop' or if very unlucky they might end up in a prisoner of war camp—such was an airman's outlook during the war. Instead they were fated to undergo a nightmare experience which nearly had a macabre ending for them all. Shot down, often betrayed on the escape line, handed over to the Gestapo, imprisoned in Fresnes where they were beaten and tortured, packed tightly into cattle trucks, they were transported to Buchenwald, or 'Forest of Beeches'—surely the most euphamistic name for the death camp into which they were clubbed and kicked by demented SS guards.

The horrendous crimes committed in Nazi concentration camps have been well documented since the war. It is still difficult for most people to imagine how it felt to be subjected to such degrading and inhuman treatment, which left permanent physical and mental scars on many survivors, even destroying some. When the airmen were released and sent to Stalag Luft III they tried to describe their experiences, but the other prisoners of war had great difficulty in believing them. I spent over a year in the concentration camps of Sachsenhausen, Flossenburg and Dachau, and so I know something of what the airmen must have suffered in Buchenwald. My experience came after I had been in normal prisoner of war camps so I was at least inured to barbed wire, but for all of us the dividing line between life and death was very thin.

The utter despair, exhaustion, starvation and death engendered by the deliberate Nazi system of brutality and sadism operated by the Kommandant, his vicious wife and the SS guards are described in horrifying detail; the murder of the gypsy children and the strangulation of the SOE agents are indelibly printed on the mind. Shafts of light relieve the blackness of this hell on earth; there is the resolute and wise leadership of the New Zealand Squadron Leader Phil Lamason, the fortitude of all airmen under the most harrowing conditions, the humour, resource and heroism of Wing Commander Yeo-Thomas (the White Rabbit) and the final miracle of the release engineered by the SOE agent Christopher Burney who, himself, narrowly escaped a ghastly death.

Squadron Leader Stanley Booker describes his first return to Buchenwald after nearly 40 years: 'No birds sang and the ghosts of the past rose up to haunt me'. I returned to Sachsenhausen with Colonel Jack Churchill in 1975, 30 years after liberation; it was, like Buchenwald, a vast, bare and silent memorial. We went into the Zellenbau where we had spent five months in death cells. The aura of evil had lingered on; I felt the cold hand of death once more on me, and suddenly the ghosts of so many tortured and murdered here seemed very close.

Should we not lay these troublesome ghosts of the past? It is traumatic, for those who experienced them, to recall the horrors of the concentration camps, but we feel we should remind the world, particularly those unborn at the time, that such things can happen in any country if freedom is not guarded.

B. A. James, Ludlow, Shropshire.

INTRODUCTION

In August 1944, 168 British and Allied airmen were herded into filthy, overcrowded cattle trucks and taken from Fresnes prison in Paris, where they had been subjected to brutal interrogation and beatings, to Buchenwald concentration camp—one of Hitler's vilest extermination centres. The orders were explicit: 'Not to be transferred to another camp' stated the transportation document. In less couched terms, they were to be eliminated.

Counted amongst this number were eleven men from Australia and New Zealand who went to war with the customary pride of country and Empire, resplendent in their fine new uniforms, and ready to dish out a lesson to Hitler and his all-conquering Third Reich. Instead, they found themselves fleeing their enemy over the muddy fields of France, relying on the goodness and fortitude of the French people.

In a collective sense this is not a book about heroes, nor of heroic circumstance. It is a distressing and true story of a group of ordinary men who were forever touched by the most horrifying aspect of any war—the evil of mankind.

This book was begun in 1987—a year designated the International Year of Peace. But for the men whose stories are told in these pages there has been no real peace. Many are still struggling to comprehend the terrible things they witnessed in their youth, and the memories, vividly emblazoned in their minds, ensure that they never know true peace within themselves. For them the war was not ennobling, and they were combatants who did not return from the war purified in spirit and soul. Rather they came back scarred and skeletal, strangers to their loved ones, their sleep pervaded to this day by terrifying nightmares.

I have presented here the stories of the nine Australian and two New Zealand airmen who, together with 157 of their fellow aircrew, made that journey into the jaws of Buchenwald. Their stories are meant to be representative of the rest—the men from Canada, Britain and the United States. Every incident in this book is factual, and the draft has been meticulously read by several of the principals to ensure complete authenticity. Some liberties have, of necessity, been taken with conversations, but these are carefully based on the actual dialogue as recalled by the men involved.

I have several to acknowledge for their kind assistance and support for what I was doing in putting this story into book form. I can never hope to repay in kind the time and efforts and open hospitality, nor their trust in allowing me to intrude in deep-rooted, personal memories and profound emotions, which gave me a very rare and unforgettable insight.

Firstly, my thanks to the Australians and New Zealanders who, without exception, gave me their stories over many meetings, and to their wives and families who in many instances learned for the first time some of the horrors their men had witnessed and endured.

Thanks also to Art and Betty Kinnis in Canada, who more than once threw their home open to their Australian visitor at short notice. Art, one of the Canadian airmen and nowadays principal motivator of the KLB (Konzentrationlager Buchenwald) Club, not only gave me immediate support, but endorsed my efforts to locate others across Canada and the United States following our first meeting, initiating a welcome flood of valuable information and anecdotes.

Other KLB members who helped me were Leo Grenon, Willie Waldrum, Dave High, Ed Carter-Edwards and Bill Gibson from Canada. Jim Hastin, Bill Powell, Joe Moser, John Crawford and Stratton Appleman of the United States replied readily to my every query, while in England Stanley Booker MBE, Ian Robb, Bill Hegarty, Ron Leverington, Reg Joyce and the late Eric Davis and Ken Chapman were undaunted in their efforts to ensure I had all the facts I needed.

For providing information and tributes, I wish to acknowledge further sources: George Mulvaney and Federal Minister Robert Tickner M.P. in Australia; Barbara Yeo-Thomas, John Marpole, Phil Bear and Kevin Murphy in England. From France, former Resistance worker Henri Theron, Madame Denise Lorach from the Musée de la Resistance et de la Deportation in Besancon, and French Ambassador Stephane Hessel. Lorie Acton at the Smithsonian Institution in Washington DC, Dr Hofmann at the Bundesarchiv in Koblenz, Germany, and Chana Byers Abells from Yad Vashem in Jerusalem all provided much-needed information. Dr Bodo Ritscher from the Buchenwald Memorial Museum also proved to be of considerable and unstinting assistance.

Two long-time chums and avid POW researchers in England,

Michael Booker and David Ray, gave me the same effusive and expert help as with my earlier books on the POW experience, while Jonathon Vance in Canada once again came up trumps with information and addresses. Author and war historian Alan Cooper was of tremendous help in London in guiding me to the correct documentary sources at the Public Records Office in Kew, while Don Charlwood, an outstanding Australian author and friend, read through the first draft of the manuscript and offered valuable suggestions for enhancing its structure and content.

I am equally pleased to thank former POW and inveterate escaper 'Jimmy' James for preparing the Foreword to this book. Jimmy, the author of the absorbing war autobiography *Moonless Night*, played an integral role in the ill-fated Great Escape from Stalag Luft III in Sagan. He was luckier than most, for he was not one of the 50 escapers callously murdered by the Gestapo in the sad aftermath of the mass break-out. Arrested as he tried to board a train near the Czech border, Jimmy was sent to Sachsenhausen concentration camp with three fellow escapers. He was later awarded the Military Cross and was Mentioned in Despatches for his escaping activities. I am doubly indebted to Jimmy for undertaking the task following the sad and untimely death of Group Captain Leonard Trent, VC, DFC, who had earlier agreed to write the Foreword. Trent was another participant in the Great Escape.

To Paul Rea, one of the most dedicated and thorough journalists I have ever known, whose unswerving desire to see proper and grossly belated justice for Australian and New Zealand servicemen wrongly incarcerated in Nazi concentration camps has seen him on a quixotic search through records worldwide, and the Ministerial halls of Canberra since 1978; this book owes its origins to you, and to a chance remark you made that I should look at the Buchenwald story. Paul is now working on his own book, a necessary follow-up to his award-winning documentary on Theresienstadt concentration camp, *Where Death Wears a Smile*. It is a great and moving cry for long-overdue justice.

Once again Carl Harrison-Ford has done a magnificent job in editing my work. And finally to my wife Pat, for her inestimable support and her readiness to convert my untidy script into beautifully typed pages; my love and gratitude.

Colin Burgess, Sydney

AUSTRALIAN AND NEW ZEALAND
AIRMEN IN BUCHENWALD

Flight Sergeant Mervyn Fairclough: Moora, Western Australia
Serial No. 427078. Buchenwald No. 78427

Flight Sergeant James P. Gwilliam: Bathurst, New South Wales
Serial No. 432355. Buchenwald No. 78423

Flight Sergeant Eric Johnston: Northcote, Victoria
Serial No. 418951. Buchenwald No. 78421

Flying Officer Kevin Light, DFM: Randwick, New South Wales
Serial No. 402447. Buchenwald No. 78381

Warrant Officer Thomas Malcolm: Hawthorn, Victoria
Serial No. 418755. Buchenwald No. 78379

Flight Sergeant Keith C. Mills: Mackay, Queensland
Serial No. 425954. Buchenwald No. 78426

Pilot Officer Robert N. Mills: Salisbury, South Australia
Serial No. 417883. Buchenwald No. 78405

Flight Sergeant Raymond W. Perry: Belka, Western Australia
Serial No. 415738. Buchenwald No. 78355

Flight Sergeant Les K. Whellum: Kensington, South Australia
Serial No. 417545. Buchenwald No. 78442

Squadron Leader Philip J. Lamason, DFC and Bar: Napier, New Zealand
Serial No. NZ403460. Buchenwald No. 78407

Flight Lieutenant Malcolm F. Cullen: Maungatoroto, New Zealand
Serial No. NZ421963. Buchenwald No. 78388

1

Into the Night

'**D**ear God in heaven, what is this place?' exclaimed the weary Canadian airman. Moments earlier, the solid wooden door of the cattle truck had been dragged open and a sudden burst of daylight had flooded the crowded, stinking interior. As he stared out into the vista that lay beyond the train the young man's face seemed to sag. He shuddered and repeated himself, this time in an awed whisper, 'Dear God in heaven!'

Squatted uncomfortably beside him on a small patch of filthy straw, Flight Sergeant Ray Perry from Western Australia took in the growing expression of horror on his companion's dirt-streaked face, and wondered if he presented a similar sight in the crushed motley of humanity. The rumpled shirt and trousers, ill-fitting on the trim, athletic frame, bore evidence of the five-day journey they had endured on a forced evacuation from the besieged city of Paris; he was soaked with sweat, covered in filth and scraps of straw, and stank of urine and faeces. As Ray's eyes swept around the other bearded faces, he finally decided that he and the Canadian would be quite indistinguishable from the others, all of whom were now blinking owlishly in the unaccustomed sunlight.

The expressions on their were rapidly changing from glazed resignation to a horrified incredulity as they stared out at their destination. They did not want to believe what they were seeing.

Immediately beyond the station platform was a high wire fence surrounding a cluster of squat factory buildings, but it was the sight of the men working within this fence that shocked the new arrivals. Emaciated men and boys with close-cropped hair shuffled around in dirty, striped pyjama-like tunics, wearily going about their appointed tasks. Stoically indifferent to anything but the frenzied shouts and unrestrained blows of the German guards, their expressions spoke of the inhumanities they had endured as they shuffled along.

A few metres from the hissing locomotive, an inadequate army of these barefooted living corpses endeavoured to haul a rough wooden cart overloaded with newly quarried rocks along a dusty incline. As they strained and dragged and pushed the cumbersome vehicle they were dispassionately flogged by two uniformed SS guards. Ferocious dogs snapped and tore at their legs, and they worked with a desperation that only fear of pain or death can induce.

Shrill cries and the guards' strident orders silenced the frightened hubbub of conversation in Ray Perry's cattle truck, and moments later three thick-set guards appeared at the open doorway, screaming at the occupants. Their faces red with exertion and anger, their tirade continued as they grasped those nearest the door and hauled them out head-first onto the concrete platform.

'Raus, schwein! Raus!' they screamed. Any hesitation in jumping from the train brought a heavy club crashing down on the body of the offender. Prisoners falling onto the platform were subjected to the kicks and lashing fists of the guards as they tried to regain their feet. A Frenchman pushing out of the train past Ray screamed in agony as a club thudded onto his shoulder and the young West Australian lost no time in swinging himself out and away from the doorway. He managed to stay on his feet and was forced to squeeze into a column of prisoners being formed along the centre of the platform. Even here they were not safe from the guards, who continued to lash out. Terrified men tried to force their way into the centre of the column, to escape the guards and their Alsatian dogs.

Eventually the train had disgorged its human cargo, and the guards had whipped their charges into a long column, five abreast. Ray Perry was nursing a painful shoulder where the end of a club had connected. Tears stung his cheeks, but he suffered the pain with mute determination.

For the mass of captured airmen and French prisoners, this display of cruelty was a stark prelude to the living nightmare they were about to enter—a place more deserving of Tennyson's line, 'Into the jaws of death, into the mouth of Hell', than that to which the words had originally applied.

The sign mounted at the station read Buchenwald—that is, Forest of Beeches. It was once a peaceful forest where philosophers such as Goethe and Schiller had sat and mused, their thoughts nurtured amid the lush tranquillity and raw-scented beauty. But Buchenwald was now a corruption, a blasphemy encircled by its centuries-old trees.

Eventually the column of prisoners was forced to move out of the station at the double, along a concrete road they would come to know as the Caracho Way, or the 'Street of Blood'.

It was 20 August 1944—a day Ray Perry would never forget, and the date and the day struck him as he shuffled along towards the gates of the concentration camp. This day of pain and realisation, of terror and uncertainty, was also Ray's twenty-first birthday.

More than three months had gone by since that fateful day when he had fallen from the skies over France, and found himself in the midst of the enemy he had flown over and bombed so many times. Earlier, back in England, there had been little to distinguish it from all the other days which had gone before—breakfast with his crew, the ops briefing at which they learned of their target, and the nervous sense of excitement as he clambered aboard dear old 'G-George'.

In the early hours of 7 May 1944, Halifax Mk III, LV 943, from 466 (RAAF) Squadron, had raced along the strip at Leconfield in Yorkshire and clawed its way into the almost cloudless night. Apart from English engineer Jack Dickens they were an all-Australian crew under the command of Ted Hourigan. This was their thirteenth operation as a crew, and the portent of bad fortune evinced by that number was not lost on them. They were part of a 149-bomber force detailed to bomb a railway marshalling yard at Mantes Gassicourt, 80 kilometres west of Paris.

In most respects the operation did not appear to be as dramatic as previous sorties, which had included four ops to Berlin. Ground defences in the target area were reported to be light, but as they headed out over the Channel, bomb aimer Ray Perry and navigator Chris Cullen talked for a short time on the less palatable aspects of the trip. They would be flying over France at 10 000 feet in bright moonlight, and the bomber force could easily be seen by German fighters.

At this stage of the war many small raids were being carried out on marshalling yards and similar objectives in north-western Europe, preparatory to the planned invasion. Twelve Halifax bombers had taken to the skies that night from Leconfield, which lay sixteen kilometres north of Kingston upon Hull, but only eleven were destined to return. Operation number thirteen would indeed prove unlucky for Ted Hourigan and his crew on 'G-George'.

Ray Perry had good visibility over the target and dropped their bombs across the line of markers, but as the aircraft swung for home it was pounded by cannon fire from an unsighted enemy fighter. Ted Hourigan threw the lumbering aircraft into desperate corkscrewing manoeuvres, but when he finally levelled out to allow his crew a chance to assess the damage they were hit again, and this time the shattered Halifax was set on fire and Hourigan ordered his crew to bale out. Perry, then a young farmer from the small inland town of Belka in Western Australia, vividly recalls the ensuing moments.

In the Halifax aircraft the escape hatch was in the floor of the plane near the front; in fact under the navigator's seat. The drill was for the navigator to tip up his table and shift his chair, put on his chest-type parachute pack, undo the hatch and jettison it before going out feet-first. As the bomb aimer, I was in the nose of the plane and went out second, followed by the wireless operator. During this time the engineer put on his own pack and also the pilot's pack for him. The mid-upper gunner could either come up front or go out at the back of the plane, while the rear gunner centred his turret to reach inside the plane to get his chute pack, then turned his turret hard to port or starboard and tumbled out backwards.

I got about half out of the hatch when the back of my chute harness caught on the edge of the hatch. With the wind dragging on my legs I couldn't ease myself back up to free myself, but soon felt a heavy foot on my shoulder which quickly solved the problem, and I was out. Not knowing how much height we had lost I quickly pulled the ripcord and was soon floating comfortably down, wondering what the future held. We were very fortunate, as the seven of us made successful landings and survived.

Ray Perry landed in a field and, bundling up his parachute canopy, harness and Mae West, headed for a nearby wood where he buried the lot under some leaves and fallen branches. Later that morning, having rested in the shelter of the wood, he approached some French people in a nearby farmhouse and, although none of them spoke English, he managed to convey his situation to them. After enjoying some bread and a cup of thick, steaming coffee, he was shown to a bedroom and told to rest. He woke at midday and was told to take off his flying clothes, watch and identity discs. Ray was then handed a pair of well-worn trousers and a shirt, both of which were too large for him, but a length of string tied around his waist kept the baggy trousers at full mast. Shoes, fortunately the right size, were produced, and finally a beret which had seen better days. He was given another small meal and then a newcomer arrived at the house, bringing with him two bicycles. Ray was instructed through words and gestures that he should pedal along behind this man, but maintaining a safe distance so they would not appear to be together.

I was provided with a French identity card and knew then that I was in with the Underground. I gathered that if any Germans stopped my guide I would, if allowed, just ride on and would be on my own again. If I was stopped, my guide would just continue on and leave me to my own devices. If questioned, I would not divulge who had helped me get civilian clothes or where I had obtained them. I knew if I was caught I would become a prisoner of war, but if the French people were caught it would be a death sentence for them.

As it turned out the cycle trip was uneventful, and even quite pleasant. The two men finally rode into the small town of Ivry. Here Ray followed his guide down a side path to the back of a house, which they entered through a rear door. They were expected, and Ray was introduced to a man and his wife, who made him understand that he was to stay there that night. The following day he was picked up in a car and once again enjoyed an uneventful trip to the village of Rouvre, where he was introduced to an elderly couple living in a petite two-storey house. As before, the couple did not speak any English, and his feeling of loneliness almost overwhelmed those of gratitude for these patriotic people.

Two days later a spritely lass of about fifteen appeared at the house, and Ray was overjoyed when she addressed him in English. From then on young Giselle visited the airman two or three times a week, and her visits were a highlight of his days. During one visit she told Ray that she had received news of Ted Hourigan and Jack Dickens; they were safe and under the care of another Underground group.

After fifteen days, on 23 May, Giselle arrived with two bicycles and told him that he was to stay with her family in the neighbouring village of Boncourt-par-Anet.

I met Giselle's parents, Madame and Monsieur Wyatt, and her younger brother Nöel. One of the first questions I was always asked was when

19

the invasion of Europe would commence. I had been to Bournemouth on leave in April and had found out that one could only get to the south coast with a special pass, so realised that the invasion would be sometime in the summer, especially as we had been bombing rail targets near the north coast of France and Belgium. I could only tell the French people that I thought it would be in a month or two.

The Wyatts' house was only a small two-bedroom home with a large kitchen, in which we had our meals, and a lounge room. Giselle was to move into her parents' bedroom while I shared with Nöel, who was also learning English. The house was on a good-sized block of land and had a wall about eight feet high all around. As there were no windows in neighbouring houses overlooking the backyard I had quite a bit of room to move about out of the house, and soon got involved in helping with the vegetable garden, which was a very important source of food. I never found out if they had a way of obtaining more rations to help with having an extra mouth to feed. The Wyatts also had an allotment of ground on the outskirts of Boncourt and there they grew more vegetables and ran a couple of goats, mainly for the milk from which to make cheese. The goats would breed and have kids which, when they got to a reasonable size, would augment the meat ration.

Life there was quite pleasant, but I had to have a French lesson every day, and in a short time I always had to speak French at the meal table. My conversation was very limited at those times, but I'd like to think that I helped the two children with their English. The Wyatts had a radio well hidden in the house and at 1 p.m. every day would listen to the BBC French news service, following which I would be informed of the main stories. Although we always referred to it as the invasion of France, they always referred to it as the 'disembarkation', and on 6 June, within a few seconds of 1 p.m., we knew that the invasion had begun. There was wild excitement in the house and a bottle of special wine, obviously saved for the occasion, was soon uncorked and glasses produced. Some friends arrived soon after and the celebrations continued into the night.

During July, Ray was informed that there were two RAF men staying with the elderly couple back in Rouvre, and it was not long before they paid him a visit. They turned out to be Flying Officer Frank Salt and Flight Sergeant Eric Davis, both of whom had been shot down after the invasion.

With Bastille Day approaching early in July, the Wyatts decided to have a small celebration. Having been a farmer prior to joining up, we had always kept ourselves in meat by killing sheep, so I offered to help with the young goat. The kid was held on a table while its throat was cut so that the blood could be caught in a dish to make black pudding. The stomach and lungs were about all of the animal that was not used. The liver, heart, kidneys, brain, and even the testicles were to be used to bolster the meat ration. On 14 July Frank Salt and Eric Davis were brought to the Wyatts' house, and another French family came to assist in the celebrations.

Following the invasion the Allies made very little progress into France, and the three airmen became increasingly impatient. They could not comprehend at that time the vast amount of armaments and equipment which needed to be transported across the English Channel before the commencement of the major offensive. Eventually they conferred with the Wyatts, asking if the family could arrange for them to be moved a little closer to the front. This was finally done, and after a fond farewell they set off with a member of the Underground and were placed in an empty house in a wood. They stayed here for an exasperating eight days, receiving occasional supplies of food, but impatient to be on their way.

On 1 August members of the Maquis (the fighting section of the Resistance movement) arrived and wanted the house, so the three men were shifted to another village. The next day another member of the Underground arrived and announced that he was to drive them to Paris, and they would soon be back in England. The trio broke into a round of cheers and slapped each other on the back. They would soon be home.

★   ★   ★

On 7 June 1944, a month after Ray Perry's aircraft had been shot down, seventeen Lancaster bombers from 15 Squadron based at Mildenhall, Suffolk, were detailed for operations against Maissy-Palaiseau near Paris. The operation would prove to be one of the most severe reversals suffered by the squadron, losing three aircraft over France and another shot down by enemy fighters over Friston as it crossed the coast into Sussex. Among the missing crews from the operation was that of Lancaster LM 575 'H' belonging to Squadron Leader Phil Lamason, DFC, the Commander of 'A' Flight.

The lanky, blue-eyed New Zealander was born in Napier on 15 September 1918 and worked prewar for the Department of Agriculture.

Handsome and determined, he revelled in the competition of school rugby, and today bears a twice-broken and misshapen nose as a legacy. His fortitude was to remain with him following his enlistment in his country's air force, and as a skilled bomber pilot operating over Europe he quickly earned the first of his two Distinguished Flying Crosses.

His first was won during an attack on the German city of Pilsen, a strategically important target in the Ruhr, in April 1942. During the return flight his aircraft was attacked by an enemy fighter and sustained damage; the hydraulics were shot away and the turret rendered unserviceable, while a fire broke out in the mid-fuselage area. In the words of the citation: 'Displaying great presence of mind, Pilot Officer Lamason coolly directed his crew in the emergency and, while two of them dealt with the fire, he skilfully out-manoeuvred his attacker and finally shook him off. By his fine airmanship and great devotion to duty, Pilot Officer Lamason was undoubtedly responsible for the safe return of the aircraft and its crew. This officer has completed 21 sorties and he has at all times displayed courage and ability.'

The bar to his DFC, gazetted on 27 June 1944, also cited continuing 'courage and devotion to duty of a high order' and 'vigorous determination' in attacks on Berlin and other heavily-defended targets.

Looking back over more than 50 years, Phil Lamason's memory of that final raid on Maissy-Palaiseau is still quite clear in his mind:

We took off from Mildenhall about 2350 hours on a bombing mission to Maissy. Our target was a bridge over the railway line, giving access to troops on their way to the front. There was some low cloud, and we flew in as the first wave of aircraft to attack at eight to nine thousand feet. Unfortunately we arrived over the target area about half a minute early, before the Mosquitoes had dropped their flares, and I throttled back, not wanting to over-run our objective. It was a bad mistake because I presented the German fighters with an easy target. They attacked, and our right wing exploded into flames. I gave the order to bale out immediately, worked my way out of my seat wearing my navigator-style chute, and jumped. Our aircraft was well alight and as I watched, it just collapsed at the wing roots and went in.

I landed in a field near Trappes about 0200 hours and hid my parachute, harness and Mae West in some bushes. I had sprained my ankle badly on landing but was pleased to come across my navigator, Ken Chapman, a few moments later. We remained together from then on. We walked across country for about two kilometres until we heard some voices. We dropped to our bellies and crawled towards the voices until we recognised the French language. We approached the group who had been watching the raid and Ken, in his rusty French, told them who we were and asked for help. But they didn't appear to be all that keen to assist us, and pointed us in another direction where they said we might find some help. Soon after, we heard more voices coming from the courtyard of a house. The two of us approached a small group of two or three families who had also been watching and listening to the raid. We declared our identity and were at once taken to a nearby house, where we were given first aid for our injuries, which were minor, a strong alcoholic drink, and a light meal.

Lamason and Chapman were given some additional food which they placed in their pockets, and were escorted to a small wood a kilometre away. They remained hidden that night, and early the next morning a boy of about sixteen brought some more food and told the two men that members of the Resistance would come and arrange to give them shelter. A little later two French women arrived, one of whom spoke reasonable English. Flying Officer Ken Chapman from Sussex remembers their first day as evaders being a combination of confusion and uneasiness, but recalls with fondness the people who risked their lives to help.

The woman who could speak English welcomed us and gave us a great deal of encouragement by telling us of the work of the French people as a whole against the Germans. She went away and returned later with the local postman, a member of the Resistance. Evidently he just wanted to look at us, but could speak no English. Again they left; we found a clearing in the wood and lay and rested in the sun. About 11 a.m. the English-speaking woman returned with the French boy, carrying a sack of civilian clothes. We gave up our battle dress for these, and although we looked a couple of tramps we could reasonably pass as a couple of French labourers to a dim Jerry.

We were to walk to a rendezvous where a car would be waiting for us. Phil, who had sprained his ankle, had great difficulty in walking the two or so kilometres through the wood. After cautiously avoiding two German soldiers repairing telegraph wires we reached the car containing the driver and his pal, who had been searching for us. The 'car' was a contraption with an engine of sorts, with a cab built of wood and numerous holes in the floor. I was to curl up in the back and cover myself with sacking. Phil, donning a beret, sat beside the driver.

The ride was anything but comfortable, and in my position I could see nothing of the countryside. We dodged a couple of German motorcyclists who threw suspicious looks at the car, and arrived at a farmhouse. Here we were taken inside to a good meal. I produced a packet of Players and our French friends went into raptures. Towards the end of the meal the son, spying at the gate, ran in to announce a car of German soldiers approaching and we had to make a hurried exit through the rear window, across the garden, and scale an eight-foot gate, which Phil found some difficulty climbing. We ran across a ploughed field, jumped into a running stream, and hid under the stump of a fallen tree. Soon our friends came to say that the Germans had called for water for their car!

The two men were taken to a barn near the house until it was considered safe for them to be driven to their first lodgings. They were covered with sacking in the back of the car, and eventually pulled up in a side street in the small town of Montfort l'Amaury. Here they were welcomed by Roger Ceuillener, the town locksmith, and his wife Yvonne. Inside the comfortable house a pleasant surprise awaited them in the shape of George Scott, an American airman. Yvonne produced some more respectable clothing and hid their personal belongings for them while they changed. They stayed with the Ceuilleners for five days, never leaving the house except to use the outside toilet, and only then with extreme caution.

One sad event during their stay was the occasion on which the entire village turned out to bury the RAF crewmen killed during the recent raid. Two of Lamason's crew, Rob Aitken and Tommy Duncan, were among those buried in the simple, solemn ceremony at the town cemetery. The villagers reverently laid wreaths of red, white and blue flowers on the fresh graves in a gesture of respect. Lamason was not to know for some months that his three remaining crew members, Gerry Musgrove, John Marpole and Lionel George managed to successfully evade capture.

George Scott left the house soon after to go to another hiding place. The three men were destined to meet again a few weeks later in less pleasant circumstances. The day after Scott's departure, and amid great commotion, a badly burned American fighter pilot was brought to the house, suffering from shock and exposure. Yvonne fussed over the young pilot (whom they knew only as Jack), applying jelly to his burns and placing him in their double bed. Ken Chapman felt bad about taking up their only other bed.

> We implored Yvonne and Roger to take our bed, but they wouldn't hear of it. Yvonne slept on the divan, Roger on the floor. Next day Roger made a steel arch affair to raise the clothes off Jack's badly burnt legs.

On 18 June an attractive blonde-haired Belgian girl named Marie, accompanied by two men, picked up the two airmen in the now-familiar motorised vehicle. She spoke excellent English and told Phil that arrangements were under way to have them taken out of France, either by aircraft or by train to Spain. With luck, she said, they would be back in England within a fortnight.

They finally arrived in the village of Rambouillet and the home of Monsieur Plumsard, whose genial wife gave the airmen a cup of black-market tea and a huge bowl of strawberries. That evening they were handed over to Claude Le Fevre, the son of their next benefactors in Rambouillet. Madame Le Fevre's husband was a commandant in the French army, but he had been captured and sent to a POW camp in Germany. A little later another airman on the run joined them; he was Flight Sergeant Dick Rowe, who had been shot down a few days earlier. Although Rowe later went his own way, he too was destined to wind up in Buchenwald.

The three airmen remained with the Le Fevres until the morning of 5 July, when they were told to prepare for another move. They gave their sincere thanks to madame, and were escorted into the country by Monsieur Plumsard to await their conveyance. Not long after the local fire engine pulled up beside them and the three men were instructed to don fire helmets and coats. Feeling terribly conspicuous, but pleased to be on the move again, the three men chatted, noting with some alarm a few bullet holes in the canvas cab of the tender, which Plumsard explained were the result of a fighter attack.

Just outside the village of Chevreuse, on the side of a hill, the fire engine chugged to a halt by the wayside, where they were met once again by Marie, together with a Monsieur Charbonnier, the village librarian. They removed the firemen's outfits and, trying to appear nonchalant, the party of five strolled into the quaint little village. After walking down a cobbled street they reached the library and paper shop, where they were greeted by Madame Charbonnier and her daughter Janine. Upstairs, they were introduced to a couple of RAF airmen and a Lieutenant Phelps of the US Army Air Force.

Conditions in the small flat were crowded, although generally amiable, but it was with a certain amount of relief that Marie arrived on 9 July and said she had to take two men to another house. Phil and Ken elected to go, and bid the others good luck.

A brisk ten-minute walk soon had them at the large elegant house of Madame Kalmanson and her two daughters Denise and Collette. After formal introductions they were taken upstairs to their room, which contained two beds. Even here they had to exercise caution, according to Chapman.

> Denise and Collette spoke English fluently, easing matters considerably. Our stay here was very pleasant and we enjoyed it. An unusual thing— Monsieur Kalmanson was 78 years old, and they did not inform him of our presence in the house. This procedure provided us with endless amusement, and we kept up a regular game of hide and seek!

The two men spent an idyllic fortnight at the house, eating breakfast in bed, sunbaking, and generally helping out in the extensive vegetable gardens at the rear. Eventually the aged Monsieur Kalmanson encountered Chapman going to the toilet, but after his initial alarm he accepted the situation quite happily and allowed the men to stay.

On the morning of 22 July word reached Lamason that they were to be moved to Paris. The girls ironed and pressed their clothes and they all shared an early lunch with a little 'bon chance' wine. The Kalmansons were genuinely sorry to see their guests leave, but understood their desire to return to England. After many tears and handshakes they set off from Chevreuse on foot in the company of Monsieur Chabonnier and a woman named Janine. They walked for three kilometres until they reached the station, where Janine bought the tickets. Marie was at the station and told Lamason and Chapman that she would take over and escort them to a 'safe house' in Paris.

The train was crowded with people, particularly poor folk from Paris who had come to the country to buy, beg or steal vegetables from the farmers. Lamason and Chapman stood patiently in the crowded carriage as the train moved slowly from the platform. The passengers had to disembark at Maissy-Palaisseau and walk to another train three kilometres away. Phil caught Ken's eye and winked. Only weeks earlier they had been above this same place, trying to blow the rail bridge to pieces, and now they had to suffer the general inconvenience inflicted by the RAF bombers. Another train was waiting at a bomb-damaged station and they clambered aboard with Marie.

Hours later the train arrived at the Gare Universite and the two airmen caught their first sight of the elegant, ancient city of Paris. Liberation, they felt, was now close at hand.

* * *

Almost without warning Jim Gwilliam crashed into the upper branches of a large tree, breaking a painful path downwards to the lower limbs. One branch caught under his parachute harness, slipped up the back of his battle jacket, and bowed under his weight. The red-headed tail gunner from Bathurst in New South Wales found himself in the ignominious situation of being suspended upside-down like a skewered apple, bobbing up and down as he struggled to hit the quick-release button. His whole left side felt numb, but self-preservation gave him strength. After several attempts he managed to punch the button with sufficient force; the parachute clips disengaged and he fell to ground heavily, landing just centimetres from a barbed wire fence. As he sat up he was surprised to note that he was wearing only his right flying boot, then he recalled the left boot becoming jammed in some twisted metal cladding in his gunner's turret. He had left it behind in his haste to leave the doomed aircraft.

He released himself fully from his harness and was relieved to note that the worrying numbness had been caused by an incorrectly positioned strap. As full feeling and the realisation of his position coursed through him he looked around in bewilderment and dismay, feeling but hardly noticing the stickiness of fresh blood on his mouth and chin. During his descent the area around his mouth had been quite painful; he'd spat out blood and pieces of teeth all the way down. Swaying beneath the silken canopy Jim could not recall hitting anything in his frantic efforts to leave the blazing aircraft. However, the loss of a few teeth did not mean as much to him as the sight of a fierce fireball which had erupted below him as their brand-new Halifax bomber slammed into the ground. Now, safe and relatively unharmed on the ground, he wondered about the fate of the rest of his crew.

As he pondered his immediate movements, the peaceful chimes of a nearby clock tower rang out, and Jim found himself headed in the direction of the sound. The delusion of peace was suddenly shattered by the howling sound of enemy fighters swooping in to land at the nearby Montdidier airfield. Jim lay low for a short time, and pulled the mandatory escape kit from beneath his jacket. They all carried this survival pack, but he never thought he'd be putting it to use. He stashed the kit in the trunk of a nearby tree, intending to retrieve it a little later. Then settling back against the tree, he went over the events of the past few hours and decided he was lucky to be alive.

It had been the first operational foray for the crew aboard the newly delivered Halifax Mk V, EY.P ('Peter'), which displayed a mere four hours' flying time on the clock. They took off from Breighton bomber station in South Yorkshire at 2236 on the evening of 21 June 1944 as part of the 4 Group Bomber Command attack on Laon, in northern France. Their skipper, Bob 'Lofty' Mills, had previously flown a single operation with another crew from 78 Squadron, and now he was taking an excited, albeit tense crew on their first bombing mission. The weather boys had forecast a low ceiling of cloud over much of England and France.

No problems were encountered as they passed over the French coast with Calais to port and headed inland. There was a little medium flak, but the crew were chiefly concerned about German fighters, which they knew were operating in vast numbers over the area. They dropped their load of high explosives and incendiaries and flew out on a sweeping reciprocal course. Not long after, mid-upper gunner Doug Foden reported to Bob Mills over the intercom that he thought he had seen an aircraft below them. The skipper dipped the port wing, then the starboard, allowing the anxious crew to scan the night skies. Nothing. Then, twelve flying minutes away from the target area, disaster struck.

With terrifying suddenness the Halifax shuddered and shrieked as .75 mm shells from a Junkers 88 raked the aircraft from below, lancing the port wing tanks. The fuel erupted into flames, which streamed out behind the Halifax's wing in a fiery, 30-metre contrail. Bob Mills gave the order for an immediate evacuation.

Navigator Keith Mills hurriedly stowed his navigation table and seat before fixing on his parachute. Together with bomb aimer Ian Innes he attempted to open the escape hatch in the floor of the aircraft, and had a few hectic moments when it jammed. Two hefty kicks finally cleared it and Keith told Ian to jump, following immediately behind.

Wireless Operator Eric Johnston was seated in the front of the Halifax, forward of Keith Mills. With the bale-out order he began to stuff some precious items down the front of his battledress. In went his thermos flask, escape kit, and a small koala bear he always carried as a good-luck mascot. Eric waited until Ian and Keith had evacuated, remaining with Bob Mills for a few seconds as the pilot initiated a steep dive in an endeavour to extinguish the fire. The attempt proved futile, so he clipped on his chest parachute as Bob scrambled out of his seat. Eric then made his way to the escape hatch, pushed himself out into the fierce slipstream, and as he fell watched with alarm the roaring display of fire and sparks above him as the tail of the aircraft rushed by. Bob Mills jumped clear moments later.

Jim Gwilliam would later be reunited with Bob and Keith Mills and Eric Johnston, but he would not know until his return from Germany in 1945 that the rest of his crew had survived. Charlie Wright, the English flight engineer on an otherwise all-Australian crew, was taken prisoner after running into a German ack-ack battery, while Doug Foden managed to evade capture until the end of the war. Ian Innes established contact with the French Underground and joined forces with them. His efforts with them would earn him a Military Medal for bravery—paradoxically an army decoration.

It had been a tumultuous few hours, but as dawn began to pale the sky Jim Gwilliam headed off once more on what he hoped might be his first steps to eventual freedom.

On the outskirts of the village whose bell chimes had attracted his attention, Jim came across a small cottage and decided to try his luck with the occupants. It was difficult sneaking up to it in his single flying boot, but he was soon beneath a window. He raised his head for a furtive glance and took in a small but cosy-looking room with a deal table, two chairs and a bunk in the far corner. A grey-haired man was stretched out on the bunk, fast asleep, his snores quite audible through the window. Raising his head once again, Jim noticed a worn shirt draped over one of the chairs, beneath which stood a pair of muddied boots. It seemed to indicate the man was a farmer, so Jim decided to take a chance on his patriotism.

Quietly at first, he tapped on the windowpane with his fingernails. Then he rapped a little harder with his knuckles. After a few persistent knocks the man's eyes suddenly snapped open and he looked around in bewilderment. It would be difficult to guess who received the bigger shock as their eyes locked through the window. The man looked in horror at the bloodied apparition outside his house and yelled in fright. Alarmed by the shout, Jim took off. After running a few paces he decided to go back, realising that he had probably frightened the farmer, and retraced his steps to find the man peering around the door. It was a few moments before the farmer took in the dishevelled flying suit and realised who had woken him. Overcoming his fear, he looked around and hurriedly beckoned the airman inside.

By now the farmer's wife was in the tiny room, clutching her clothes to an ample bosom as she anxiously looked on. Her fear subsided a little when her husband explained their unexpected guest's identity. Jim picked out the words 'Ahr-aye-eff' in the excited dialogue, but she was still wary as she invited him to sit at their table. Then she examined the young airman's blood-streaked face. She clucked a little, left the room, and returned with a water-soaked cloth, with which she cleaned up most of the encrusted blood and grime. He was given a small cup of milk, which he drank gratefully, and a welcome cup of strong black coffee. The farmer's wife cut him a thick slice of bread, which he gingerly chewed on as he tried to communicate with his benefactors.

The small village was named Le Tronquoy, and as they began to explain where it was located another man suddenly strode in through the door. He took in the stranger sitting at the table and immediately broke into an animated discussion with the farmer and his wife. The young newcomer was quite suspicious and sat on the end of the bunk, lighting a small pipe as he eyed Jim Gwilliam and his flying clothes. At one stage he pointed the stem of his pipe at the wing-encircled 'AG' insignia on Jim's jacket and asked what was a fairly obvious question. When Jim responded by pantomiming his role as an air gunner, the fellow looked at him with fresh interest. It seemed the newcomer was not family but was a resident in the house. After a short conference they indicated to Jim that he should sit tight while the men went out to retrieve his parachute. He pointed out the direction he had come from and the two Frenchmen set off, returning half and hour later with the parachute bundled up in an old hessian bag. Their arrival was timely; as they walked in the sound of a Focke-Wolf filled the air for some minutes. It was sweeping low, obviously searching for parachutes in the trees.

The husband and wife became quite agitated and the younger man was still uneasy with Jim's presence. The penalty for harbouring escaping servicemen was death, and though Jim was still feeling giddy and tired from shock and the smashing blow to his chin, he declared his intention of moving on. They all looked considerably relieved at this, and saw to it that he was well provisioned for his journey—with a little food and a battered pair of sturdy brown work boots. Although reluctant to venture out into open territory once again, Jim bade them a gratitude-filled farewell and set off.

As he walked along in the morning sunshine, an incautious lethargy crept over Jim Gwilliam—in all probability a traumatic reaction to recent events. Whatever the reason, he found himself wandering without concern down a road heavy with passing traffic, caring little for the German tanks, motorcycles and pushbikes as they passed by. Despite the fact that he was wearing an RAAF uniform with flight sergeant insignia and the word 'Australia' on his shoulder tabs, it can only be assumed that the Germans, inured to a vast array of uniforms throughout Europe, did not even give him a second glance. Of course no one would expect an enemy airman in full uniform to walk along a main road in broad daylight.

When the realisation of his folly suddenly hit Jim, he snapped out of his torpor and quickly dashed off into a nearby wheatfield, running heavily through the chest-high crop. Moments later he blundered into an unseen obstacle and fell heavily. His tumble was accompanied by outraged oaths from the naked couple whose lovemaking had been so violently disturbed. Jim quickly leapt to his feet and fled the scene as the flustered man continued shouting at him. Jim saw the funny side of the incident and a mischievous grin crossed his face. But running up a rise into a clump of trees he suddenly stopped dead in his tracks and his smile vanished. Right in front of him stood a massive, camouflaged German Tiger tank.

The shock of the unexpected confrontation quickly disappeared when it became apparent the tank was unmanned, and there were no Germans in the vicinity. The whereabouts of the tank driver was a mystery, although Jim feels he may have been the upper portion of the coupling he had so rudely interrupted. He had taken little notice of the language used by the man, merely the threatening tone. Inspired by this good fortune, he pressed on.

> In the distance I could see a small village, and I moved onto the road which ran towards a small cluster of outlying houses. I was more cautious now, and slowed my pace as I reached a tree-bordered bend on the outskirts of the village of Cuvilly. My caution was justified; just around the bend four German lorries were parked and two of the drivers were enjoying a smoke. Another pair were relieving themselves in a small ditch by the side of the narrow dirt road, not 30 metres from where I stood. I did an immediate about-face, but as I walked past a two-storey cottage I noticed a woman staring down at me from an upper window, her hand over her mouth in astonishment. She knew exactly what I was. Following this I made a wide circuit of the village, finally withdrawing to the temporary shelter of a huge elm tree on the outskirts of Cuvilly, where I contemplated my next move.

The serenity was shortly broken by the unmistakable sound of a Merlin engine passing overhead. As Jim peered through the foliage of the elm a solitary Spitfire passed to the north of Cuvilly at about 5000 feet. His predicament came to him more potently than ever; in just an hour or so the lucky devil in the Spit would be back at base, enjoying a hot brew with his mates. Jim's stomach rumbled at the thought, but he settled down on the grass and began to nod off.

The rustling of footsteps woke him with a start, and he looked up with alarm into the face of a teenage boy. The lad spoke to Jim, who indicated that he did not understand French. Through the boy's gesticulations he understood that he was to stay put, and the lad left Jim to ponder this new situation. For all he knew the youth might give him away to the nearby Germans. On the other hand, he needed to contact someone he could trust and who could pass him on to the Underground. The boy, he decided, was as good a start as any.

A short time later the youth returned on a pushbike and urged Jim to straddle up behind him once they got onto the road. The youngster turned out to be the son of the woman who had earlier noticed him on the road. The ride was uncomfortable and awkward, but Jim felt that at last something was happening. He managed to enjoy the scenery throughout the 20-minute ride, during which they skirted back around Montdidier. Fortunately they did not pass any enemy soldiers. The bike finally crunched to a halt outside a huge house, where they were welcomed by an attractive woman in a simple cotton dress. After a brief exchange the young guide told Jim to enter. The house was sparsely furnished. An ornate, polished staircase swept upwards to a second level.

The woman was an English schoolteacher whose late husband had owned several cafes in the devastated Pas de Calais area. Over the next four days Jim was able to relax a little. A maid fixed his meals, and he caught up on a lot of missed sleep. He was supplied with a smart set of civilian clothes, and his uniform was taken away and carefully hidden.

The owner assured Jim that plans were under way to help him, but he must remain hidden. On the fourth day he noticed a suspicious character hanging around the house and told the woman. She became quite agitated and made arrangements for him to move to another house. That night the young lad took him to a smaller house beside the main road leading into Cuvilly. It had been recently ransacked, and the doors and drawers had been forced open by bayonets. Outside, all manner of German personnel and vehicles passed directly by—all within a couple of metres of the house. It was not an entirely comfortable situation, but every day the maid brought him some food and reassured him in broken English that things were well in hand for his return to England. Apart from her brief daily visits Jim was alone during the long days and nights and he began to grow anxious; it was only a matter of time before someone came snooping.

On the fourth afternoon ne noticed a suspicious character across the road, then at eight o'clock he heard a muted knocking at the back door. His heart pounding with trepidation, Jim opened the door, and in barged his young friend, closely followed by a small crowd of wild-looking, all members of the Maquis and armed to the teeth. These rugged individuals were soon dispersed around the small room, talking in low but animated tones. Some came over and shook Jim's hand, muttering words of assurance, while others thumped him heartily on the back. Thunder rumbled outside, and heavy drops of rain began slapping at the dusty windows. Finally it was dark enough to move out, though by now the rain had intensified and occasional sheets of lightning illuminated the room and its occupants with startling clarity.

As thunder boomed all around them, the Frenchmen began turning up their collars and shouldering their Sten guns. The young lad came over to Jim and said 'We go now!' The prospect of walking out into a fierce electrical storm filled the Australian airman with dread, but he understood the urgency of the situation and reluctantly followed the Frenchmen. The sky was alive with ripping sheets of lightning, while thunder crashed and rolled menacingly. Feeling cold and miserable, Jim plodded through one of the most terrifying nights of his life.

Even today I refuse to go outdoors when it rains; that's how bad it was, and how badly that shocking night in the French countryside affected me for the rest of my life. Storms absolutely terrify me now. But eventually we reached the outskirts of a small village named Ployron where I said goodbye to the blokes from the Maquis. I was still trembling from the walk, but managed to wave goodbye and thank the men. Not long after an elderly peasant came along on a horse and dray and pulled up. The youngster led me to the dray and told me to climb up beside the old man. Once I was settled in the seat my young helper wished me 'Bon chance!' and shook my hand. I owed him so much, but by the time I had begun to thank him he'd already started back the way we'd come. The old man smiled at me and said 'Bonjour monsieur', than he clicked his tongue at the horse and we moved off.

The storm abated, and the sun was soon trying to peep through some scattered clouds. The old peasant appeared to be dozing, so Jim relaxed, enjoying the freshness of the air and the tranquillity of the passing countryside. An hour later the horse pulled up at a small house by a rail siding, which appeared to be the gatekeeper's cottage. The old man indicated to Jim that he could get down, and as he did so a slim attractive woman in her mid-thirties opened the door, looked around and waved him inside. He had to duck his head as he entered a cosy, well-furnished room. While he waited for the woman he looked around, and with a start noticed three small photographs propped on the sideboard. They were the escape-kit photos of three of his crew—Bob Mills, Eric Johnston and Keith Mills. The photos, taken back in England, showed the men in civilian clothing and were intended for use in making fake passes.

Jim could barely contain himself as he called the woman over and pointed at the photographs, then at himself. 'This is my crew,' he said. 'These men are from my aircraft!' The woman smiled widely. 'Oui monsieur, je comprend. Attendez monsieur, attendez.' She then showed him into a small room and as he slumped onto the single bed he gratefully shed his sodden boots. He was exhausted after the adventures and dangers since landing on French soil a few days earlier. As he removed his jacket he heard the front door close, and then the heavy clump of footsteps in the next room. He heard voices, and his door suddenly opened. Framed in the doorway was a huge, moustachioed Frenchman in a check shirt and flannel trousers. Having ascertained that Jim did not speak any French, he introduced himself in broken English. His name was Pierre, and he revealed that the others on the crew had been at the house but had since moved on. He did not know their current whereabouts, but said he would try to find out. Jim thanked Pierre, who smiled broadly through his bristling moustache. He was a big brute, over two metres tall, and he really had to stoop low as he left the room.

Over the next few days Jim spent much of his time both in and on the small bed, waiting for any news. Pierre visited once or twice a day to bring food, but his news was always the same—wait. German rail trucks and other armaments were constantly clanking past the small cottage, but the guards on board paid little attention to the dwelling by the rail siding.

Several days later Jim was dozing in his room when Pierre entered. He apologised for the intrusion and then, lifting the cover, began to search for something beneath the bed. 'Excuse me,' he said, dragging out a heavy, cloth-covered bundle. 'I must bury somewhere.' To the Australian's amazement the bundle was unrolled to reveal several Bren guns, grenades and boxes of ammunition. He had been sleeping on top of this little arsenal for a week! Pierre rewrapped the bundle after carefully checking the weapons, gripped it in his massive arms, and after a further apology calmly strode out.

Later that day Pierre took me to a neat farmhouse a quarter of a mile up the road, where I was greeted by a French couple who invited us in and gave me some bread and wine. They did not know where the other three men were hidden, but promised to ask around. The husband happened to tell me that the crash site of our aircraft was quite near, and asked me if I'd be interested in looking at the wreckage. I said I would, and we all walked to a small clearing nearby. On the edge of this clearing, with broken bushes and fresh mounds of dirt everywhere, lay our once beautiful Halifax. It was just a twisted, broken heap of scrap metal. I really felt quite sad as I looked over the remains of what had been virtually a brand-new aircraft, and Pierre was most sympathetic. He said 'C'est dommage, monsieur. Quel gaspiage' (Such a shame, sir. Such a waste). None of us spoke a word as we returned to the farmhouse.

Over the next few days Jim enjoyed some very pleasant times with the family, and often played cards with their young daughter. Sometimes they had visitors, and Jim was instructed not to speak to anyone. Pierre told him that the visitors assumed his guest to be mute. Nobody paid particular attention to him in the time he spent at the farmhouse.

Then came some welcome news. Keith Mills was in the nearby village of Coivrel, and arrangements were being made for him to pay a visit. Later that day he was picked up by a young farm worker on a pushbike and doubled along the narrow dirt road. They passed several Germans on the way, but were left alone. Though dressed in peasant clothes, Jim had taken the precaution of wearing his perforated metal identity tags concealed beneath the collar of his shirt. These tags were commonly known to aircrew as 'dead meat tickets'; if killed, the tag was removed and forwarded to Allied headquarters so relatives could be notified, and the wearer's death recorded. In Jim's case, it was the only means by which he could identify himself as an airman, should he be captured. He knew that any serviceman captured in civvies could be executed as a spy, and the knowledge made him more than apprehensive.

Finally the young farm labourer pedalled into Coivrel and pulled up at a small corner cafe. They dismounted, strolled over to a battered door, and knocked. The door swung open, revealing an elderly man with a trim white moustache. He greeted the youth, sized up the stranger behind him, and then urged them to enter. Inside sat Keith Mills, who leapt to his feet and shook Jim's hand vigorously, and launched into a gleeful barrage of questions.

Later, when the excitement had died down, the two crew members sat at a round table over coffee brought to them by the diminutive grey-haired Madame Tempez, wife of the cafe owner. Keith told Jim that the elderly couple had been very good to him and had not asked him to leave even when it was discovered that a local, known to be a collaborator, had started asking questions of his benefactors. The previous evening the collaborator had been intercepted and escorted out of town by a small group of villagers. They returned soon after, but the collaborator did not. No one spoke of his fate, but it seemed certain he would never betray anyone again. Keith's other news was of a Lysander aircraft being organised to pick them up, along with Bob Mills and Eric Johnston, who were apparently being sheltered nearby.

Though anxious to see his friends again, Jim had to contain himself while cautious arrangements were made, and the next five days passed slowly for the two Australians in their small room above the cafe. Monsieur Tempez kept them supplied with food and coffee, occasionally chatting to them about his hobby of rabbit breeding. From time to time they could hear German voices in the cafe below, but they were never disturbed.

Finally the evening came when the two airmen were taken to meet Bob and Eric, who were hiding in a small dwelling at the rear of a large house on the other side of the village. The property was owned by the patriotic Mayor of Coivrel, Monsieur Omnes, and here a joyful reunion took place. When all the back-slapping was over the four men settled down around a polished antique table and began to take stock of their position. Everything seemed to be going so smoothly now, and Jim looked forward to their return flight.

On 28 July, the men were told the Lysander would soon land at a nearby location. At noon the following day a petrol-driven covered truck squealed to a halt outside the Mayor's house. Bob and Eric made their farewells and climbed into the back, where two young Frenchmen were already seated. The truck rumbled around a few corners and pulled up outside the cafe, where Jim and Keith piled in, each clutching a bottle of local wine.

They headed off in a westerly direction as the six men in the covered cabin at the rear chatted happily and drank from the bottles. Outside the sun was shining, and the Australians' mood was almost festive. They were on their way home, and with a bit of luck would be in England for breakfast.

The truck stopped briefly on the outskirts of Maignelay where one of the young Frenchmen, Ronald, wished everyone good luck and clambered out. Ten kilometres on the truck pulled over to the side of the road and one of the two men in the driver's cabin came around the back, beckoning the airmen to follow him. It was a pleasant day for a hike, and the four men and their guide strolled through a thin forest and across some fields at an easy gait. On their way they saw the top half of a stationary locomotive just over a distant rise. Their guide told them that it had been there for some time after being severely damaged by Allied fighters.

Eventually they entered a thick wood where the guide said they should make themselves inconspicuous, stating he would return in a while with another vehicle. The four men sat down and enjoyed some cigarettes, eagerly discussing what they would do once they'd reached England. About an hour later a horn tooted a prearranged signal and they made their way onto the road, where a small black sedan with two men in the front was waiting. They were told to squeeze into the back seat and were assured that the trip would only be a short one. Uncomfortable but happy, the Australians watched as the lush country-side swept by.

Suddenly their mood changed from elation to alarm as the driver swung around a corner and drove straight up to a roadblock. A squad of German soldiers ordered them out of the vehicle and told the men to raise their hands. A further surprise came when the boot was opened and another man scrambled out carrying an automatic rifle, which he quickly trained on the airmen.

Once they had been searched the men were handcuffed and ordered back into car. An armed soldier covered them from the front seat and the sedan roared off again, this time following another car. After a long trip suffered in silence they were driven into the forecourt of Beauvais gaol.

They had fallen into a trap laid by a local collaborator who had given them up to the Germans. The Australians were stunned but at the same time deeply concerned; they hoped that reprisals would not befall any of the kindly villagers who had aided them over the past few weeks.

The captured airmen underwent interrogation, at which time they were informed that, having been captured in civilian clothing, they had given up their status as prisoners of war. Eventually they were taken to Fresnes prison in Paris for a further bout of interrogation. All four had begun their nightmare journey to Buchenwald.

2

Betrayal and Capture

It was Monday, 24 July 1944. The air-raid sirens began wailing as Phil Lamason and Ken Chapman sat uneasily on a wooden bench in the heart of occupied Paris, waiting to be picked up by their next contact in the escape line. They looked up, hoping to see some Allied aircraft, but none seemed interested in flying over the French capital that day. Parisians largely ignored the sirens and scampered about on their daily business. A few metres from the bench stood a nervous Frenchwoman, the helper who had brought them to this spot. She waited and watched as well, but she was observing the pedestrian traffic, looking for her contact or for any signs of trouble.

On their arrival in Paris two days earlier the Belgian girl Marie had guided Phil and Ken to a two-storey house in the Rue d'Assass, overlooking a school by the magnificent Luxembourg Gardens. Here Marie had handed them on to their next hosts, the Werths. Despite the acute shortage of food in Paris, Madame Werth had provided them with good nourishing meals.

After a pleasant weekend Madame Werth guided the two men to their next rendezvous. She rode her bicycle a cautious 100 metres ahead of the airmen, who strode after her until she arrived at a small bench where she indicated they should wait while she watched from a discreet distance for the next link in the Underground chain to appear.

The air-raid sirens were still sounding when a portly Frenchman strolled over to Madame Werth. They talked for a few moments and then she beckoned the two airmen over. Then with obvious relief but tears in her eyes, she wished them a safe journey and indicated they should go with the man, named Georges Prevost. As they watched Madame Werth remount her bicycle she smiled, crossed her fingers as a sign of good luck, and pedalled away.

The routine was the same as before. They followed Georges Prevost at a safe distance as he walked towards yet another place of hiding. They crossed the Seine at the Ile de France, enjoying their first sight of the magnificent Notre Dame cathedral in spite of their precarious position. Next they passed the Prefecture, the Palace of Justice, and entered the Rue de Sevastopol. A few brisk strides took them to an apartment opposite Demoy's Restaurant, and they followed Georges up a narrow flight of stairs to the top flat. Here they were greeted by a young, short and fair-haired man wearing thick-lensed glasses, who introduced himself as Captain Jacques, an officer in the French Intelligence. He assured Phil and Ken they were now on the final stage of their journey and would soon be back in England. As Lamason recalls, the contact's words were quite heartening.

> This man claimed to be working for the chief organiser of the escape route to Spain [the Comet Line]. He had a detailed story of how the journey would be accomplished, and claimed to have made the journey seven times.

The two men relaxed and were all smiles as they were introduced to George's sister Genevieve. Ken Chapman felt quite at ease and remembers every effort being made to ensure their comfort and make them feel that they were safe and among friends.

> We had good meals here and had a comfortable double bed to sleep in. We were given clothes to wear so that our own could be pressed, and we could go out onto the balcony overlooking the Rue de Sevastopol to watch the throngs of people go by. Georges and Jacques provided us with tobacco, so we were fairly well supplied. That night Georges and Genevieve came in with two bottles of champagne, which we soon disposed of!

The following day Jacques returned to the flat with a young RAF evader identified only as Bob. Later, while conducting a question session, Jacques asked the three airmen for the names of those who had helped them in their journeys across France. Immediately all three became suspicious, and Lamason asked Jacques why he needed such delicate information.

'Many of these people are very poor and need money,' he explained. 'If you prefer not to tell me their names it is all the same to me, but it is usual for us to show our gratitude by rewarding such patriotism with an amount of 200 francs for each day you were with them.'

It all seemed perfectly reasonable. Jacques' credentials and authority seemed to be in order, so the three men divulged the names and locations of their past helpers. The following day Lamason and Chapman left the apartment building with Georges and Jacques and were handed over to Jacques' assistant, an unpleasant-looking woman with copper-coloured hair and spectacles. Jacques would not divulge her name, but they later discovered she was known as Madame Orsini. She took over responsibility for the welfare of the two airmen and guided them along the banks of the Seine, through the beautiful gardens of the Louvre, and on to the Place de la Concorde. Here they waited for an hour until they were picked up by two men in a black Citroen. Both spoke perfect English with strong American accents.

The passenger in the front seat, who reminded Lamason of a Hollywood gangster, introduced himself as Jacques' chief in the Resistance network. He was a tall man of 80 or more kilos, with brown hair and blue-grey eyes. Lamason's first impressions were actually borne out when he told them something of his background. In response to their surprise at being picked up by agents who seemed to be Americans, he claimed to have lived in Chicago for twelve years, and to have known Al Capone!

His driver was an even taller fellow in his mid-twenties. A ruggedly good-looking man, he had fair hair, blue eyes, and bore a faint scar along his forehead, just below the hairline. He told the men he had been born in California and had joined the French air force in 1939. In what appeared to be an easy conversational manner he tried to cajole Lamason into a discussion of the comparative air defences of Britain and Germany, but the New Zealand squadron leader was non-committal and would not be drawn into talk on such a provocative subject.

They drove past the Eiffel Tower and pulled up in front of a block of flats near La Foret Boulogne. Here the two airmen were temporarily separated, Lamason in one room and Chapman in a small children's bedroom. On the surface, things seemed to be going smoothly, but Chapman was beginning to feel somewhat ill at ease with their situation.

I felt terribly lonely, and I had plenty of time to think. Swastikas were scrawled on the walls and to me this seemed strange. However, the tall American came in and reassured me.

41

That night the two evaders shared an uninspiring meal before retiring, although the news that they would be on their way home the following day brightened their outlook. Both spent an uneasy night wondering about what the morning would bring, and the hours crept by until it was time for breakfast. Ken made his way downstairs, where he found Phil already chatting away with six other airmen, who were moving in, prior to their departure for Spain and freedom. The hours now passed quickly.

It was not until lunch was over that their move was fully organised. Ken Chapman was to ride on the back pillion of a Frenchman's two-stroke motorcycle to the prearranged rendezvous, while Lamason was to go by Metro with another Frenchman. They set off, and just after two o'clock were reunited at their rendezvous near the Champs-Elysees. Both men were dubious about the wisdom behind this move, as they now found themselves almost directly in front of a German barracks, and the area was swarming with enemy guards. Chapman takes up the story:

> We were left in the company of my escort. We crossed the road to a cafe and ordered some beer. Meantime we watched the passers-by. Many German troops were passing, but no private vehicles. All French people used cycles, of which there was a multitude. At 1500 hours I paid the bill and we returned to our rendezvous point across the road. A quarter of an hour passed and no one had arrived, and I was uneasy—there were too many Germans about who might recognise us for what we were.
>
> Soon two strangers came up, shook hands with our guide and with us, and led us to a car. We got in and thought we were at last on our way. We drove some five minutes then suddenly entered what later proved to be Gestapo headquarters with two guards outside! We were covered by guns, removed from the car, and led up several flights of stairs to a room where we were searched and handcuffed together. Our Frenchmen had betrayed us, and we were in the hands of the Gestapo.

Almost two weeks after Phil Lamason and Ken Chapman had unwittingly fallen into enemy hands, Ray Perry, Frank Salt and Eric Davis were driven into Paris by their Underground helper. Their journey was incident-free and they were told they would be placed into safe houses over the weekend. Subsequent plans called for them to be picked up and taken somewhere south of Paris. Here they would be given passage aboard an aircraft secretly bringing in supplies for the Maquis, which would take them back to England. Ray Perry picks up their story:

> After Frank and Eric were dropped off our guide took me on the Metro to the suburb in which my house was situated. I had one nerve-wracking experience when we were crammed in a carriage on the Metro and a German soldier, speaking in French, asked me what the time was. Having been warned not to speak to anyone I thought quickly enough to show my left wrist, on which there was no watch. Much to my relief he immediately turned to someone else and asked them the time.
>
> I was duly picked up in the car on 7 August which, besides containing Frank and Eric, also had three Americans, two of them being on the floor in the back. As it was then only early afternoon our Underground friend said he would take us to see some of the sights of Paris, so we drove around the Arc de Triomphe and passed the Eiffel Tower before driving through a narrow archway off a street into a courtyard where we stopped. The driver immediately jumped out, pulled a revolver from his pocket, and told us this was Gestapo headquarters and we were now prisoners of the Germans. We didn't want to believe it as we got out of the car, but knew by the number of armed German soldiers that our dreams of being back in England that night had suddenly turned into a nightmare.

★　★　★

Warrant Officer Tom Malcolm from Hawthorn in Victoria was the bomb aimer on Lancaster LM 571 (JO.E) which had taken to the skies on 24 June 1944 as part of a 112-aircraft attack on the Prouville Road junction, a heavily defended V-1 site five kilometres to the north-west of Bernaville in the Pas-de-Calais area of northern France. The aircraft, from 463 (RAAF) Squadron, was flown by the affable Pilot Officer Tony Martin, a former gold refiner from Mount Lawley in Western Australia.

Moments after dropping their bombs on the target area their aircraft had been set upon by swarms of fighters. The Lancaster burst into flames, and a few moments later exploded. By incredible good fortune Tom Malcolm was already wearing his parachute and was blown clear of the aircraft; the rest of his crew were killed instantly. Despite the shock of the explosion he had enough sense to pull the ripcord as he hurtled through the night sky. After landing he set off, hoping to meet some friendly French people who could put him in touch with local members of the Resistance.

43

Tom eventually arrived in the large town of Beauvais, 70 kilometres to the north-west of Paris. He had passed through Flanders Field, where, in that summer of 1944, the fields were blanketed with sweeping beds of the famous red poppies. Beneath the flowers and green grass lay the muddy earth in which Australian and New Zealand and other Allied troops had fought for so long and so desperately nearly 30 years before. At almost every road junction he passed small graveyard plots filled with white crosses bearing the names of French or Allied servicemen, each generally surmounted by a simple shrine above the well-tended graves. The sight of shattered houses along the way served as a further grim reminder of the war.

Once in Beauvais Tom drifted into an ancient cathedral, where he decided to gamble on asking for help from a pleasant-looking woman sitting passively in a wooden pew near the altar. At first she was startled when he addressed her in English; although they were the only occupants of the church she was decidedly uneasy. However she indicated that he should stay where he was while she went to seek the assistance of some friends.

Left alone to ponder his fate, Tom actually dozed off, and woke with a start when the woman returned in the company of a tall Frenchman. The man began firing questions which Tom answered, apparently to his satisfaction, as he then identified himself as the captain of the local Maquis. He took Tom to a nearby house where he was shown to a cellar filled with rack upon rack of dusty bottles of champagne. The Frenchman swept his hand around. 'Console yourself when the bombers come,' he said, with a twinkle in his eye. 'And if they don't come, console yourself anyway!' With that, he was gone. His words were quite prophetic. The bombers did come not long after, and explosions shook the cellar floor as the nearby railway yards were devastated. The Australian needed no further urging and, uncorking a bottle, he consoled himself! As Tom Malcolm explains, his path to freedom was soon organised.

The Captain arranged transport to Paris in a furniture van and, after a few miles, the largest of my fellow passengers enquired if I was English. I said 'Yes' and waited. He told me that the others had decided I was, and as we were to be stopped just outside Paris by the Germans, for the checking of identification cards, it would be advisable if I concealed myself. I followed his suggestion and under cover of a few boxes and coats managed to pass through the roadblock. My large benefactor turned out to be no less than Monsieur Thieblemont, chief of the Beauvais gaol. He had been in a similar position in the Paris gaol, but didn't suit the Germans. I went with him to his house, still within the walls of this Paris gaol, met his wife and daughter, received more French greetings, and spent my first night in Paris in gaol!

Monsieur Thieblemont had contacted my Underground address and after a stroll round Paris in the morning I met the man who was finally to place me with the 'Organisation'. This was Monsieur Girand, a quiet little grey-headed man who spoke perfect English and soon escorted me across Paris to his home. From there I moved to several different apartments in Paris, always under the noses of the Germans. The ordinary, happy young people who watched and risked their lives for us were known as the 'Pericles' Resistance group.

On 19 July 1944 Tom Malcolm was transferred once again, to the house of a portly policeman named Georges Prevost, where four American airmen were already hiding. It was at this apartment Tom and the others first met the young man calling himself Captain Jacques, who told them he was with the British Secret Service.

Having questioned all of the airmen to his satisfaction, Jacques informed them they would be driven to the south of France by truck. Elated with their apparent good fortune and impending freedom, Tom and the others started talking eagerly about what they would do once they reached England.

A short time later Jacques called back and told the waiting airmen that a truck had been organised and was waiting at a fixed rendezvous. The five men followed Jacques down the street, walking briskly behind him along the wind-swept footpaths bordering the Seine. All around him Tom could see historic buildings and colourful shop facades, and he revelled in the feelings of excitement and wonderment at the passing pageant of wartime Paris. Along the banks of the mighty river he saw some plane trees with their white bark scarred (or perhaps glorified) with the Cross of Lorraine. When they arrived at their rendezvous, Jacques motioned his charges into the back of the truck, closed them in and then climbed into the driver's cab with a large, fair-haired man wearing an ancient leather jacket. Inside the rear of the truck were another thirteen men—all of them airmen on the run.

As the truck moved out into the light traffic, the eighteen men in the back settled down in anticipation of a long, uncomfortable ride. A couple of them had expressed some uneasiness at the news that they would be driven to southern France. They had been warned back in England not to accept rides in petrol-driven vehicles as gasoline was strictly rationed, although German collaborators were known to have a ready supply. The argument was dismissed in light of their confidence in 'Captain Jacques'.

A few minutes later the truck pulled up and the motor was switched off. The men had no idea what was happening until the two doors at the rear of the truck were suddenly thrown open to reveal a brace of Germans armed with machine-guns. It was a crushing blow for Tom Malcolm and his dismayed companions.

> Our truck was in an enclosed courtyard, strangely enough called the Court of Sausages, and most of the available artillery was trained on us. Our friend Captain Jacques had cleverly passed us on to the Germans. Thus ended my chance of escape at that time, and the joys of life under the Nazi heel were to be mine for a few months.

*   *   *

It becomes necessary at this point to tell a little of the history and deeds of the so-called 'Captain Jacques'. This man, responsible for the capture of dozens of fugitive airmen, was actually a double agent in the employ of the Germans.

Jacques Desoubrie, to give the man his real name, was the rotten apple situated at the end of a long line of brave but unsuspecting patriots, and he had been operating successfully as a German agent for some months under the aliases of Jean Masson and Pierre Boulain. 'Captain Jacques', as he liked to be known, was responsible for the capture of the majority of the 168 airmen who later ended up in Buchenwald.

Born in 1921 at Tourcoing on the Belgian frontier, Desoubrie was the illegitimate son of a Belgian doctor. Never having a proper home, and abandoned by his mother at an early age, he became a drifter and later took up a trade as an electrician. When war broke out the Belgian teenager eagerly swallowed the Nazi propaganda, readily adopting their doctrines. He foresaw a worthwhile occupation as a collaborator for his new masters, and soon became a key figure in the French Underground, passing valuable information back to the Gestapo. In April 1943, he was recruited as a guide for the Comet escape line, on the Brussels to Paris section. Little did the French Underground workers realise that Desoubrie, who received large sums of money from the organisers of the Comet Line to assist evading airmen, belonged to an elite Gestapo team headed by the infamous Prosper Desitter.

Desitter and his mistress Flore Dings worked with Masson/Boulain/Desoubrie to destroy the Comet Line in Paris during 1943-44, and successfully penetrated other Allied escape lines. Desitter would inject members of the German Abwehr into the Underground system, disguising them as evading airmen, and was responsible for sending an untold number of evaders and members of the Resistance into Fresnes prison in Paris, and often to their death in one of Hitler's concentration camps.

Jacques Desoubrie's favourite ruse in gaining confidence with unsuspecting Resistance workers was to pass himself off as a British agent, and he was reported to have conspired in many dozens of betrayals. He was responsible for the arrest of around fifty French and Belgian Resistance workers, almost all of whom were executed.

A short, stocky man with piercing grey eyes set behind a pair of moderately thick-lensed spectacles, Desoubruie dressed quite smartly, and his light brown hair was always immaculately combed. An easy smile revealed bright gold fillings in his front teeth. Many an evader was taken in by his excellent English, oily charms and smooth reassurances. His assistant or secretary, was a waspish woman known as Madame Orsini. Thin and short, she had a sallow complexion, copper-coloured hair and wore dark-framed spectacles. Following the fall of Paris, Desoubrie stabbed Orsini so she could not tell of his traitorous activities. Unfortunately for him she did not die, and following some intense questioning by Allied interrogators she was imprisoned at Fresnes for sedition.

Once Desoubrie had penetrated the Comet Line and established himself with many of the Resistance workers, more and more British and Allied airmen were gathered in by his smooth charms. He laid his intricate web with ease and his operation, in fact, was remarkably easy. The airmen were placed in convenient apartments or hotel rooms where they were promised rapid despatch to Spain or England. The people who gave them this information were genuine Resistance workers living in fear of discovery and execution, so their anxiety and precautions were very real.

Desoubrie would then interview the evaders and, before their suspicions were aroused, try to learn as much as he could of their activities, their background, and the names of those who had helped them. He would then send cars or small buses to the hideouts and the generally trusting airmen would clamber in, eager to be on their way. It seldom crossed their minds that they had been sold out to the Germans, who simply gathered in the victims as they were delivered directly into their hands at Gestapo headquarters in the Avenue Foch.

Other evaders fell prey to similarly unscrupulous collaborators who had infiltrated the Resistance. These traitors were everywhere, and through the French Milice—a paramilitary force of fascist collaborators—the Gestapo would lull their aircrew victims into a false sense of fraternity and security. In many cases the airmen became incautious and talkative. A favourite ploy of the Milice was to have one of their men burst into the room where an unsuspecting airman was undergoing an apparently harmless interview. The Frenchman, one hand bandaged and ostensibly wounded, would blurt out in outrage that there had been an ambush and one of the so-called airmen had to be a German traitor. The situation was both dramatic and unnerving in its presentation.

Once the distraught man had been calmed down and ushered out, the concerned interrogator would point out that the integrity of the airman before him was easily resolved. Just a few answers to some 'harmless' questions that no German could possibly know, and this would quickly establish his bona fides. Nothing of a military nature, of course, just everyday things such as the name of the pub favoured by the lads in his squadron, their favourite beer, the name of the publican, and what one would see when looking south from the bar. Harmless stuff indeed, but once such information was passed on to the German Intelligence officers at the Dulag Luft interrogation centre at Oberursel, it could have a demoralising effect when casually mentioned to a newly captured airman from that squadron. The airmen asked to supply such 'trivial' information were generally more than willing to talk in order to demonstrate their innocence in the matter of the purported 'ambush'.

Jacques Desoubrie served his masters particularly well, but his traitorous actions were finally uncovered. Suspicions were aroused when scores of evading and escaped airmen entrusted to his care mysteriously vanished from the normally secure Comet Line. Following

Squadron Leader Philip J. Lamason, DFC and Bar.

Flight Sergeant Ray Perry.

Warrant Officer Tom Malcolm.

Prior to capture, three airmen destined for Buchenwald pose with their French benefactors, the Wyatts, Bastille Day 1944: Eric Davis (second from left at rear, Frank Salt (centre, with tie) and Ray Perry on right. Madame Wyatt at front left, son Noel in front of Eric Davis, and daughter Giselle between Frank and Ray.

the war 'Captain Jacques' was put on trial in Lille under his real name. He was found guilty of collaboration and treason, and executed in the winter of 1946. But that was in the future. In the months before the Allies finally swept into Paris, Desoubrie was the man who presented his alleged credentials to the airmen, and they were completely taken in.

Although many of the airmen in Paris were duped into giving the names and addresses of those who had aided them in France, Belgium and Holland, it was fortunate that they gave this information to Desoubrie and his henchmen after D-Day. With the whole of Paris in turmoil, the Germans had enough on their plates without worrying about rounding up hundreds of relatively harmless villagers across France. This was especially true after the attempted assassination of Adolf Hitler on 20 July, when members of the Gestapo were arrested and dumped into an already overflowing Fresnes prison. The bloodbath that followed undoubtedly saved many of the airmen from the brutal interrogations conducted in the Avenue Foch. Several airmen and Resistance workers still fared badly at the hands of the Gestapo, but given the general confusion following the invasion, the bungled assassination, and in the face of an anticipated assault on Paris, it is probable that many might otherwise have been tortured to death.

There are many stories and reports from the airmen who were rounded up and despatched to Buchenwald, and most of them demonstrate the extent to which the Gestapo had infiltrated the French Underground. Flight Sergeant Les Whellum from South Australia is one who can attest to the scale of the deception.

Whellum was a wireless operator with No. 102 Squadron. His Halifax III, under the command of fellow South Australian George Mulvaney, was shot down near Beauvais on 28 June 1944. After a time he managed to locate some members of the French Resistance and soon felt he was on his way back to England.

> I had been at a woodcutter's house for a few days when word reached me that I was to be moved on quite hurriedly. I was rather disappointed, as arrangements had been made for me to meet up with my skipper, who was hiding up in the village of Becquet St Paul, fourteen kilometres away towards Beauvais. But questions had been asked around the village recently, and it was generally feared that a collaborator was trying to locate our whereabouts.

A battered truck called at the house the following day, containing two other Allied airmen being evacuated from the area. The truck headed southwards, making for the Gisors area, from where we were told we would ultimately join an escape route through Paris. Along the way we encountered two German roadblocks, but these did not present any undue problem. We were all dressed as French peasants, and we simply got out of the truck and ambled past the roadblock as the truck proceeded and was searched. The Germans were most methodical in searching any vehicles that reached the roadblocks, but did not worry about anyone walking through. Once out of sight of the Germans we simply jumped back in the truck. It was strangely exhilarating to stroll so casually by our enemy who did not give us a second look.

Sadly, my bid for freedom came to an end at George Prevost's apartment in the Rue de Sevastopole, at the hands of Captain Jacques. The three of us joined several other British and American airmen at the flat, from which we were eventually taken in pairs, ostensibly to a new address, but in reality to Gestapo headquarters by Jacques' secretary.

A random group of MI9 reports prepared postwar by many of the Buchenwald airmen further reveal the extent of corruption in the escape lines at that time.

Flight Sergeant Edward Phelps, 207 Squadron, RAF:
I was taken by car to a flat somewhere in the outskirts of Paris where I stayed for two days with three men and a girl. A well-dressed man tried to pump me for information by asking me to fill out a spurious Red Cross form. On the Thursday he said I was going to be driven to the Spanish border. I got in a car, but was driven straight to Gestapo headquarters.

Flying Officer S. A. Spierenburg, 582 Squadron (DFF), RAF:
I was staying in a house when I was introduced to a man called Jacques who moved me to another home. Later I was taken to the Hotel Etoile and stayed there for three or four days. On 14 July another man came to the hotel and told me to get ready to go to Lyons. We went out to the car and I realised by looking at the driver that I was in the hands of the Gestapo. I was taken to the Palais de Securite, and then to Fresnes.

Flying Officer Stuart Baxter, 514 Squadron, RAF:
A Monsieur Jacques came to the flat and told the three of us [all from

the same crew] that he was English and a member of the Secret Service. He interrogated us as to our true identities and said he would get us to Spain. He told us he would send his secretary to collect us. At 1500 hours a woman arrived and took us by car to Gestapo headquarters.

Flight Sergeant Terry Gould, 10 Squadron, RAF:
At the end of our six weeks' stay in St Andre I was moved in the company of three Americans. We were moved by car to Paris where we were all driven to a private home. Here we found about 20 Allied personnel and all of us were told that we should be moved in the direction of Spain the next day. We were all fed that night. The next afternoon we were taken out, being told that we were to meet our transport at six o'clock. At six we met this transport which collected 33 of us altogether. To our disbelief, we were all driven straight around to Gestapo headquarters.

Flying Officer Douglas Percy, 630 Squadron, RAF:
I stayed in the house of a man who kept the local garage in the village of La Villeneuve en Cherie. I met three American airmen at the house. On 28 July our host handed us over to a guide who took us by car to Paris, where we were taken to a house. There we met Squadron Leader Lamason and his navigator, who told us they were leaving that day and everything seemed all right. When it came our turn to be taken out of Paris we were stopped, asked for our identity papers, and taken to Fresnes prison.

First Lieutenant James Hastin, 374 Fighter Squadron, USAAF:
American Air Force Sergeant George Scott and I were moved to the Post Office in a nearby town where some people said that we would be flown out. There was a lot of confusion about where the plane was going to pick us up. We should have smelt a rat here because we were taken by car to the town together with two English chaps at a time when the only people driving cars were the Germans. We were then taken to Paris, to meet with some other people, and to wait for news of our plane. After a meal we were taken to the Piccardy Hotel, where we stayed for three days. While we were there a man who spoke excellent English came and asked us to complete Red Cross forms. On these forms were a lot of trivial questions, such as marital status, name of mother-in-law, do you own a dog, and so forth. But there were also questions relating to the type of aircraft you had flown, where your

51

group was stationed, the missions you were on when shot down, and others. It was a standard type of Red Cross form that the Germans used, and which we had been briefed on back in England.

On 28 June a French-Italian chap came and told us to be ready to go in five minutes. He was going to take us to Orleans, as our plane had been cancelled. He gave us papers saying we were Belgian workers. Sergeant Scott, plus one of the RAF airmen and I got into the car and we drove off in the direction of Orleans. However, we were stopped at a roadblock and asked for our papers. A couple of Germans got into the car and proceeded to search us. One of them found my dog-tags, and that was it for us. We had been sold out.

Flight Lieutenant Peter Taylor, 158 Squadron, RAF:

The man who said he was working for the British Intelligence was called Robert Moulet. He fetched me from the chateau on about the 27 April 1944 and took me to a village called Breteuil, leaving me in a cafe owned by a Monsieur Duboille. Here I met two other RAF types named Sergeant Downdeswell of the same squadron as myself, and Sergeant Hegarty of Snaith RAF station. We stayed here for about a fortnight. Moulet then fetched me and took me to a small village called La Chaussee de Bois De L'Ecu, where he left me at the house of a family called Anty. I stayed here for about two months. By this time our invasion had started and they said they had instructions not to try and get people away, but to wait until the British overran the place. On 28 July a representative of Moulet came and asked me if I would like to fly to England. I naturally jumped at the chance and we set off for Moulet's place in the nearby village called Caply. On the way we picked up two American airmen who appeared to be waiting; they were Lieutenant Hunter and Sergeant Edge.

After a short journey Moulet stopped and a little later a car drove up with two civilians in it who told us they were going to take us to the plane. All three of us boarded the car which finally struck a main road and set off towards Beauvais. We had not gone far before I saw another car parked at the side of the road with two men tinkering with the engine. They signalled us to stop, and when we did so we were surrounded by armed Germans, and that was that!

3

Fresnes Prison

The vast Fresnes prison, nearly 20 kilometres south of Paris, and close to the present-day site of Orly Airport, was built in the late 1890s. When completed, it comprised three massive blocks or divisions, each containing five storeys of cells, and was the largest criminal penitentiary in the country. But as German troops swept into Paris the SS replaced the incumbent police guards with their own men, and the cells were soon filled with political prisoners.

Entrance to the prison was gained through a set of heavy gates off the main road to Paris, then driving down a cobbled private road through an avenue of magnificent poplars until reaching the main gate. Here twin statues of the Sisters of Mercy were positioned either side of the huge iron gates. However many of the men and women despatched to Fresnes were only too well aware that mercy had very little place in the SS doctrine, unless it was the swift mercy of a bullet.

The majority of prisoners were French, although some were from the occupied Channel Islands, gaoled for sedition and non-cooperation. Several British subjects, a small number being secret agents, were also held in the stark cells. Among the agents imprisoned there were Odette Samson, who was held in solitary cell 108 in the 3rd Division, and later cell 337; Peter Churchill in cell 220 in the 2nd Division; and Wing Commander F. F. E. Yeo-Thomas in cell 293, also in the 2nd Division.

Division One was for male prisoners of the SS and Wehrmacht, usually German deserters. The second was also for males—Frenchmen, political prisoners, agents, saboteurs and other categories. Division Three, in which the airmen were held, was a mixed block holding both men and women.

The cells, measuring four by two and a half metres, had stone walls partially covered by crumbling plaster, into which were scratched dozens of messages proclaiming both hope and despair. A large frosted glass window, through which thick bars could be seen, was set high in the wall opposite the steel door. Beside this door sat a lavatory, a tap, and a small enamel basin secured to the wall, as well as a wooden shelf and pegs to hang clothing. A single bed frame lay folded against a wall. When this was lowered a shapeless palliasse served as a mattress.

The prisoners were inspected through a small oblong slit and spy hole set into each door. The majority of cells had no lighting, and prisoners were checked by guards shining a torch through the inspection slit. In those cells which had lights supplied, they were kept on all night.

Over several weeks the captured airmen were delivered to Fresnes prison, transported there in company with French prisoners, and sometimes one or two fellow aircrew. They were not to know for some time the actual number of airmen sent there, nor the enormity of the deception that saw so many picked up through the actions of double agents and traitors such as Jacques Desoubrie.

On arrival they were taken into the nearest building, where their handcuffs were removed. They were counted as they entered, and found themselves in a long, broad corridor where the walls rose to an arched ceiling four storeys above their heads. Each floor was indicated by a narrow steel balcony, secured to the concrete walls by stays and bolts. These were connected vertically by steel ladders, and horizontally by slightly arched walkways which spanned the chasm between balconies at each level.

Next the men were shepherded into a series of small wooden cubicles from which they were eventually taken one at a time, made to strip naked, and thoroughly searched. The guards confiscated their belts, ties, shoes, matches and the contents of their pockets. It was here that most of the men had the dogtags ripped from their necks by guards shouting abuse and calling them 'terrorfliegers' (terror flyers). Any signs of disobedience or defiance brought a savage blow to the head, or a swift kick to the shins with a heavy jackboot. Flying Officer Kevin Light, DFM, was kept in one of the wooden cubicles throughout the day following his arrival. He filled some of that time carving his name and service number into the wall with a small knife. At a time when Bomber Command crews could take their discharge after 20 operations Kevin had decided to continue on, and had flown an extraordinary 53 operational sorties before being shot down. As he carved his name into the wooden wall he had time to reflect on the events which had brought him to this place.

Educated at Marist Brothers' College in Randwick, New South Wales, Kevin Light enlisted in the RAAF in July 1940 and received his initial training at Bradfield Park before attending Empire Flight Training School in Edmonton, Canada. Arriving in England in March 1941 he became a Navigation Officer with the RAF's 142 Squadron, then operating on Wellington bombers.

One tragic night, during a training exercise at Binbrook field in misty rain and poor visibility, he was involved in an horrific crash. The crew's usual skipper, the well-liked Billy Brill, was operating as second dickie to another pilot who was experiencing great difficulty in landing a near-new bomber on the repaired strip. At his third attempt the man came in too high and thumped it down halfway along the strip. The Wellington raced off the end into a field, and as the pilot desperately hauled it into the sky once again it became evident they would hit a cluster of trees. The lumbering bomber tore a path through the topmost branches, gained some altitude, and then began to plunge uncontrollably to starboard. It finally banked to vertical and Kevin Light knew their pilot had lost control.

The doomed aircraft rolled beyond the vertical, arched towards the ground, and then slammed into a field, tearing in two and erupting into flames on impact. Kevin Light came to with his hair and jacket smouldering, and the air around him full of noise, thick smoke and fire. Somehow he fought his way out of the twisted fuselage, slapping at his hair and jacket as he made his way outside, where he collapsed with shock. A young soldier, quickly on the scene, hauled him to safety and he was soon being treated for his wounds. The other six were killed in the crash or subsequent fire.

Kevin could have opted to resign from the force but he decided to stay on, and entered an air gunnery course. His next posting was to the illustrious 9 Squadron, then he transferred to No. 460, and finally arrived at 12 Squadron. Along the way he picked up a well-deserved Distinguished Flying Medal and a new bride—his English sweetheart Brenda, an attractive WAAF from Derbyshire. They had been married for only five weeks when he and his Lancaster crew under F/O Jim Smith took off on Kevin's fifty-third and final trip over enemy territory.

It was the evening of 18 April 1944 and their target was the railway marshalling yards at Juvisy, south of Paris. Flying too far south of the area, Smith made a late run over the target well after the other bombers (including some from the famed 617 'Dambusters' Squadron) had dropped their bombs and headed for home. They managed to release their load of bombs but were hit by flak. The aircraft began to blaze fiercely and break up as Smith told his crew to bale out. Moments before it exploded Kevin Light managed to hurl himself out into the night sky and parachute to earth.

His story of evasion across France over the next few weeks is similar to that of many of the other Buchenwald airmen. After landing he made his way to the village of Longjumeau (Seine-et-Oise), where he asked for help and was taken into the house of the mayor, Jean Rodier. He stayed with this family for eighteen days before heading south, teaming up along the way with an American evader. Several weeks later they fell in with a group who claimed to be Resistance workers. The two men were taken into Paris and lodged at the Piccadilly Hotel, but to their misfortune they had fallen into the clutches of Jacques Desoubrie, who questioned the airmen and then delivered them to the Gestapo.

Soon after Kevin Light had carved his name into the wall of the cubicle at Fresnes, he was taken out to be searched and interrogated. He was then placed in a cell with an American flyer, where they were later joined by an English pilot whose arms had been badly burned when he was shot down. The man's blackened hands continually oozed pus and he was suffering from shock, but the Germans ignored all entreaties to give him any sort of medical treatment. Eventually, to the relief of all, he was removed from the cell and his burnt hands received some attention.

★   ★   ★

Every prisoner entering Fresnes had a story to tell. When Mervyn Fairclough was brought to Fresnes some weeks later he was placed in the same cubicle as Kevin Light to await questioning. Mervyn, from Moora in Western Australia, had been shot down following a bombing run over Tergnier. The crew, from 51 Squadron based at Snaith in South Yorkshire, had been ordered to bale out by skipper Mervyn Hall, but only three were able to do so. After hiding out with some sympathetic French families Mervyn was sold out to the Germans by a traitor in the local Underground, and captured on a road near Beauvais. After the war he received a letter from one of his French helpers informing him that the traitor had been 'dealt with'.

It was with some surprise that the West Australian saw Kevin Light's name scratched on the wall of the cubicle, as the two men had trained together back in Australia. The familiar name gave him a welcome uplift of spirits. Afterwards, when searched, he was wearing a gold ring on his right hand, engraved with his name and that of his wife Elaine. He protested loudly when a guard began to wrench it from his finger, and for his trouble he received a stinging blow to the face. The guard slipped the ring into his pocket, then spat on the airman and hurled abuse. He grabbed Fairclough's arm and sent him on his way with a kick to the back of the legs.

Eric Johnston was carrying his small, furry koala mascot—a good luck charm he had risked his life in retrieving from the cockpit of the doomed Halifax before baling out. At Fresnes a guard seized the mascot, dropped it on the floor and deliberately crushed it beneath his heavy jackboot. Eric Johnston gritted his teeth and glared at the man, but wisely held his tongue. His silent insolence was still enough to earn him a sharp belt across the mouth.

Jim Gwilliam found himself locked in a cell with an Englishman sporting an angry-looking sty on his left eye. Once they got around to talking his companion revealed that he had been picked up in a brothel, where he had earlier been placed by the Underground. He told how he had taken advantage of a little carnal delight by peeping through keyholes as the girls cavorted with their clients. Jim prudently refrained from asking the fellow if he thought the sty was a form of penance for his voyeuristic activities.

Very few of the airmen who entered Fresnes prison escaped brutal physical beatings and the constant threats of death. The living conditions were totally degrading, while the food was both appalling and irregular. The tiny cells were overcrowded, there were no facilities for exercise, no contact with the outside world, and the men were forced to wear the same clothing throughout their imprisonment. Fleas, lice and other bugs thriving on filth were an incessant source of aggravation. Like the other prisoners the airmen were forced to clean their cells daily.

There was a much-feared torture chamber in the basement, where the men were sometimes taken to be beaten and questioned, then left naked in a cold, dark cell for days or even weeks. More than this, however, the inmates feared the trip up to Paris and the notorious Gestapo headquarters.

Prisoners called out for interrogation were placed in a long black maria vehicle and transported under escort to Avenue Foch. These trucks had small windowless compartments either side of a central corridor. Prisoners were locked into the cells where a tiny wire grille provided the sole means of light and comfort. An armed guard sat on a folding seat below the wire-covered rear window and kept close watch on the cell doors.

Gestapo headquarters were located at Nos. 82 and 84 on the Avenue Foch. An elegant building with ornate iron gates, it had once been a private residence—a stately home on one of the most picturesque, tree-lined avenues in Paris, which runs from the Arc de Triomphe to the greeness of the Bois de Boulogne. The illusion of nobility soon vanished as one entered this building, for the principal activities at No. 84 were interrogation and torture.

Members of both sexes were at the complete mercy of the Gestapo torturers. Those conducting the interrogations wore civilian clothing and performed their task methodically, stopping only when they had learned enough, or had caused the death of their victim. If the primary interrogation was considered unsatisfactory further beatings, whippings, burnings and submersion in icy water followed. Fingernails and toenails were torn from their sockets. The genital region was a particular favourite for the attention of the interrogators, and often the mere threat of severe and even permanent damage brought the desired response from their victims.

Second Lieutenant Jim Hastin, USAAF, had been picked up after hiding out in the notorious Hotel Piccadilly. The young pilot, from 374 Fighter Squadron, was shot down on 8 June 1944 while on his seventieth mission, his second for the day. Among the effects he had when turned over to the Germans was a towel he had taken from the hotel. A French barber called in to give some of the Fresnes prison inmates a haircut noticed the towel and asked the American if 'a red-headed woman and a Belgian wearing a leather jacket' had brought him into Paris. He further asked if a short man wearing rimmed glasses had been responsible for his arrest. When Jim confirmed all of this the barber shook his head and said, 'Then you were sold to the Germans!' He went on to say that the identities of these people were known, and they would pay at the time of liberation.

Flying Officer Thomas Blackham, DFC, from Dunoon in Scotland, was shot down long before D-Day while on a raid over France. He managed to keep the aircraft flying until all his crew had baled out safely, and then a sudden explosion knocked him senseless, hurling him through a glass panel. He recovered consciousness to find himself surrounded by flames and jumped clear moments before his aircraft blew up. Parachuting into Maquis country, the young airman narrowly escaped being hanged as a German spy. Fortunately another British airman in the vicinity was able to vouch for him.

For months Blackham lived and fought with the Maquis, until he was sent on to Paris for return to England. He too was betrayed by Jacques Desoubrie, and was eventually imprisoned in Fresnes. He recounts some of the maltreatment he received at the hands of the Germans—particularly the day he was in a group which faced a firing squad manning a machine-gun, and he looked squarely into the faces of the men who could end his life.

That machine-gun was never fired. The Nazis were master craftsmen in mind torture [and] they left us standing for several hours. All the time the three Germans were preparing the gun, and every moment we expected to hear the order given for them to shoot. Instead we were hustled off to the prison dungeons, stripped of our clothing and put under cold showers. Some of the group were very feeble and one old Frenchmen next to me was on the point of collapse. I spoke to him—and was hit over the head by the Nazi guard. He hit me with a filthy broom. The wound it made festered and my throat afterwards swelled so that I could only eat and speak with much pain.

Each one of us was then put into a cage-like steel wire locker with no room even to raise an arm. After leaving us there for some time we were 'gently' interrogated about our Resistance comrades. We told nothing and, after one or two more questionings at intervals, I was separated from my fighter pilot friend and other prisoners, and put in a cell by myself. Throughout the night I could hear men and women screaming as they were tortured. From there I was moved into another cell—all part of the ceremony to make me talk—with a little Frenchman who had been terribly tortured. He had been whipped with knotted thongs and the knots had broken two of his ribs. It was an agony for him to breathe.

I was here for two weeks, living on weak sauerkraut soup and sleeping on filthy lice-infested straw. The lice, however, provided a useful diversion; we spent much time betting each other how many of them we could catch in a given time. Neither of us received any medical attention, but by this time my throat had healed quite unexpectedly.

Unlike the majority of airmen swept up by the Gestapo, Malcolm Cullen was a fighter pilot. From Maungartoroto in New Zealand, he flew Typhoons with No. 257 (Burma) Fighter Squadron. On the night of 24 May 1944 six of the squadron's Typhoons had joined forces with eight others from 193 Squadron, with whom they had been engaged for several weeks in pounding the invasion coastline from west of Cherbourg to east of Amiens. Their objective had been a large concentration of camouflaged petroleum vehicles in the rail sidings south of Amiens. His aircraft was hit by flak as he flew out of the target area and, after gliding to a safe landing in a field near a small forest, he fled his blazing fighter for the safety of the woods.

He spent several weeks on the run, living with sympathetic families across France, but ended up in Paris, where he too fell prey to Jacques Desoubrie. Cullen and an American Marauder pilot were placed in a 'safe' flat and questioned by Desoubrie, following which they were told they would be driven elsewhere. Instead they ended up in the clutches of the Gestapo. His cell in Fresnes contained a Frenchman and, as he would soon discover, thousands of bed-bugs.

As I was spreading the rough palliasse on the floor I noted something which cheered me immensely. On the wall, scratched into the soft mortar, was the name of an American with his service number and the annotation 'USAAF'. I don't remember that name; I wish I could, for it was that which made me straighten up my shoulders and grin. I wasn't the only sucker—others had been caught. I laid down and tried to sleep, but as soon as I hit the blanket I had thrown over the palliasse they were onto me—all over me—and I must have caught a hundred before I fell asleep. I didn't sleep long, but spent the early morning scratching. When finally the light started through the bars I stood up and made an inspection around the cell, and of myself. I received a shock; I must have been bitten in at least 300 places. Great white welts stood out all over my body, and around the area covered by the top of my trousers they were almost touching.

That day I was shifted first to a shower and delouser, and from there to the fourth floor where I was extremely relieved to be greeted in my own language. There were two others in the cell when I entered, one French and the other American. The American informed me that he had been there for close on five months and he could not understand it. Others had come in and been sent to Germany within four weeks. I hoped fervently that I would fall under the latter category and made up my mind to settle down and wait with all the patience I could muster.

The days slipped slowly past, each with its own small diversity. Every day we received news of the outside world from Frenchmen who went out on working parties. This was conveyed to all and sundry by the heating system which ran up the inside wall of the cells. Each had an opening into this pipe about seven feet up the wall, and by climbing up onto our one and only stool we could shout into this primitive means of communication and receive our replies. The cry of 'Avez vous du nouvelle?' (Have you any news?) could be heard every morning. This was not the only method however. Morse code was used to a large extent, and with a spoon in one hand to make the 'dits' and a small piece of iron in the other hand for the heavier 'dashes' news was passed along the whole floor.

Stanley Booker, a 10 Squadron air observer on Halifax bombers, came from Barnsby in Yorkshire. He and several others had been hiding out in the Hotel Piccadilly, near the Arc de Triomphe, and had also been duped into capture by Desoubrie. At Fresnes he was searched, questioned about his false identity card (supplied by Resistance helpers), given a fierce beating and locked away in solitary cell 429, on the upper floor of the 3rd Division of the prison. He picks up the story.

Each day was the same—the soup trolley on its noisy track made the same noise as it approached your cell down the long metal corridors. Monday or Sunday, there wasn't really anything to distinguish one day from another. Rumours prevailed; life after D-Day was much easier as there was so much activity, and the Allies had set foot on the continent and were approaching Paris. Fresnes was an anti-climax. Having overcome the initial shock of being shot down and established a new pattern of life as an evader it came as a profound shock to be caught, given a thorough beating up—not the nicest experience when you can't retaliate—and thrust into a dark, bare cell; confused, angry, and wondering just what was going to happen next. All the time you were thinking of your loved ones at home; every day you wondered how they were taking the fact you were missing; praying, willing yourself somehow to communicate just the fact that you were alive—eager, anxious to return.

The early days were in many ways the worst—alone with your thoughts. The shock came when the German guard threw open the cell door and shouted in a pitched, hysterical way, 'Tribunal—raus!' Then down the many staircases from the upper floor, down through the maze of underground corridors and out into the open, to be shut up in a very confined metal cupboard in the special black prison coach, and driven across Paris to the dreaded Avenue Foch. Then the awesome experience of being gathered as a bunch at the foot of a vast staircase, guarded tightly, watching the hapless, bleeding and battered prisoners dragging themselves down, or being dragged down the staircase to take their place in the line, suffering from the effects of their interrogations. The apprehension, wondering how you will react; the dreadful responsibility of knowing the names and locations of those brave families that have risked so much to give you—a complete stranger—shelter and food and clothing, and take terrible chances in escorting you in trains and public transport. Now their lives are in your hands—not a happy situation!

The hours spent afterwards back in your cell, nursing your hurts, your pride, and wondering what the next 'tribunal' would be like and how you would be able to react. As the days passed and the call didn't come, a hope was cherished—perhaps they had forgotten about you. And then all is shattered, and the screaming voice again destroys your little silent world; 'Tribunal—raus!'

After D-Day things began to get a little hectic in Paris, and obviously they had to follow a different policy as the pressures grew and the Allies approached Paris. Whether you were called to interrogation probably depended on what documents or other compromising materials one carried when caught. The Gestapo were always sensitive about forged papers, especially identity cards which, although they could be stolen, had to be authenticated somewhere. I was unfortunate because, apart from a set of forged travel papers with my name and photograph, I had been given a large sealed envelope when I left my little Resistance group. I was supposed to hand it over when I made rendezvous that night with the aircraft that had allegedly been organised for me. What the envelope contained I don't know to this day, but it certainly was a source of interest to the interrogators, which didn't make life any the pleasanter at the time.

In retrospect, I wonder whether the actual beatings were perhaps not as bad as the periods of sheer fear, when your imagination runs wild in the confinement of your cell, nursing your aches and pains, wondering if the next visit would involve the real specialist torture for which the Gestapo had a reputation amongst the prisoners in Fresnes. Perhaps I came off lightly, with only two missing teeth, a badly busted nose, and a painfully swollen groin—an area to which a particularly sadistic interrogator paid very unwelcome attention.

Other men suffered severe cruelty, pain and torture during their time in Fresnes, and the terrifying sounds of men and women screaming and sobbing rent the air at all hours. Canadian Leo Grenon was hit murderously hard on the head with a Luger after being kept in a death cell for seven days, during which time he was extensively beaten. Postwar treatment for his physical afflictions took ten years, and medication was required until he died in 1994.

Another Canadian, Bill Gibson, spent 30 days in solitary confinement, with food every third day. Whenever gunfire was heard in the courtyard the guards would tell Gibson he was next for the chop. Another two of the Canadian contingent would also suffer permanent legacies of their time in Fresnes: Don Leslie lost his two front teeth, while Art Kinnis had his right eardrum broken, and did not receive any treatment for shrapnel wounds in both legs.

Airmen tossed on their bunks and pondered the awesome question: would they be next? Slowly they began to shed weight with their inadequate diet, but more than anything it was the precariousness of their position that caused the greatest anxiety.

As August progressed news of the approaching Allied armies raced through the prison grapevine. As well, the men were sometimes able to pick out a snippet or two of news from the rough squares of German newspaper the guards supplied for use as toilet paper. The prisoners began to allow themselves a little hope when reports put the American 3rd Army under General Patton at Chartres, while others said they were moving in on Versailles. The Free French forces under General Leclerc were also said to be nearing Paris. Much had to be rejected as hopeful exaggeration, but one thing was abundantly clear—Paris would soon be liberated.

In the early hours of 8 August the corridors suddenly came alive with a babble of voices and the strident screaming of the guards. The airmen's hearts sank. Evacuation could be the only reason for such mass activity so early in the morning, but surprisingly they were not amongst the first evacuees selected. Soon the din died down as the evacuees moved out, and each of those left behind breathed a sigh of relief. The Americans were coming, and they would all soon be free.

*　　*　　*

The final evacuation of Fresnes took place on Tuesday, 15 August—a hot, sticky and hazy day over Paris. Worried that roads and railways leading out of Paris would be cut before they could evacuate their prisoners, the Germans decided to give this task priority. They stormed into the prison and emptied the cells of the civilian prisoners first, packing them off to the nearby railway yards for transportation. Ray Perry remembers the day well:

> Our 'cafe' and food arrived at breakfast time and at about 9 a.m. a guard came along and informed us that we were being moved and to be ready to go at any moment. We knew then that the evacuation of the prison had been going on for some hours. Soon after our food was delivered we could hear shooting going on downstairs and it didn't take too much imagination to think that the prisoners were being taken downstairs and shot. I think we all had the same thoughts and an uncomfortable silence fell among us. Soon after being told we were to move out the shooting stopped and this relieved the tension somewhat. It was not until some time later we found out the shooting was some of the guards having revolver practice.
>
> Most of the windows were now either opened or broken and from a shouted conversation the three Americans sharing my cell discovered that their first and second pilots were also in the prison and soon made their presence known. I heard Frank [Salt] calling my name and discovered he was okay in a nearby cell on our floor. At about 11 a.m. (we had no watches) we were taken from our cell and lined up on the staging outside. There were already about 20 chaps there and we could not help laughing at one another's clothes as there were all sorts from well-tailored suits to the cheapest of peasant-style clothing, with many berets in evidence. Some had not had haircuts for weeks, and one must remember that in those days it was short back and sides, with a haircut every two weeks in the forces. Many had beards coming along nicely

and I had not shaved for over two weeks nor cleaned my teeth in that time. It was ten days since I had used soap for a wash, and after ten days in the hot cell we all had a good dose of BO.

The airmen were among the last to be taken out and assembled in the covered quadrangle. Each man had assumed that there might be some others in Fresnes, but as more and more bewildered faces emerged into the daylight the surprised shouting and conversation swelled as men recognised friends and fellow crewmen and realised the number of fellow aircrew who were in the same predicament. As a result of their sojourns to the Avenue Foch many bore black eyes and facial wounds, but they had come to regard these as symbols of their defiance, and they even laughed at each other's bruises. Finally 168 airmen, not one in uniform, were formed into some sort of order under a guard of 70 armed Germans.

A slender Prussian SS officer made his way to the front of the group and asked if any of them could act as an interpreter. A Dutch pilot from the RAF named Spierenburg hesitated, then stepped forward, and the officer addressed him for two minutes. Following this the officer turned on his heels and strode off, leaving the Dutchman to relay his message.

'We are going to be taken across Paris by bus, and placed on a train for our next destination. He did not say where this would be. I was instructed to tell you that anyone attempting to escape will be shot, and a hand grenade will be thrown into the back of the bus he came from. He has further told me to stress that he is very serious, and no attempt should be made to test his word.'

A few minutes later vats of thick bean soup were wheeled in and ladled into bowls. As the men chatted and ate the welcome soup a column of prisoners was escorted to a waiting green and yellow bus. Among those forced to squeeze aboard was the bulky form of Georges Prevost, his face now pale and drawn. Several airmen wondered if he and his sister had been in some way responsible for their betrayal to the Germans. The sad truth was that Prevost had also been taken in by Desoubrie, and when his usefulness came to an end he and Genevieve were turned over to the Gestapo. Neither he nor his sister survived the concentration camps to which they were sent.

As this bus roared away from the prison another two pulled up and the first batch of airmen was ordered to climb aboard. Soon both 20-seaters were full and a contingent of armed guards on each kept a close watch on the occupants as they were shuttled in batches to the Gare de l'Est station. They did not enter the station itself, pulling up instead at the nearby Pantin freight yards alongside a long train of French cattle trucks.

Hundreds of prisoners were milling about and the guards were kept busy shoving them into the dank trucks. The women had been segregated and were placed in five separate cars at the rear of the train. More than 30 of the cattle trucks were linked together with some carriages and guards' vans, forming a train 400 metres long. Wooden placards on the side of each boxcar stated '40 hommes/8 chevaux en long', but this restriction to 40 persons or eight horses was completely disregarded by the Germans, who crammed as many as 100 prisoners into each car. A 20-litre water pail sat in the middle of each car together with an empty one intended for use as a toilet. They were British-manufactured canisters dropped from Halifax bombers, containing food and supplies for the Resistance, and the irony was not lost on the airmen. Once again the prisoners were informed that any attempt to escape would be punished by death, and then each was given a small hard loaf of bread commonly known as knackerbrod.

The attitude of the SS guards towards their prisoners was made abundantly clear when Squadron Leader Lamason tried to protest about their treatment. For reply he received a hard punch to the face. Surprisingly, one of the elite guard responded readily to the American pilot Jim Hastin when he asked about their destination.

'You are all being sent to a labour camp in Germany,' Hastin was told. 'That is as much as I am able to tell you. But you are an American, no? I don't understand why you choose to fight against us. In the next war America will be fighting with us against the verdammt Russians!' Jim was about to reply when another guard's rifle butt propelled him towards the door of his boxcar. The airmen were loaded into three cattle trucks behind those carrying the women.

Very lights flickered in the sky to the west and south, and the distant sound of artillery reached the men as they reluctantly clambered aboard the last train to leave Paris before its liberation. During the day more busloads of prisoners reached the station to join the general melee, and were crammed into the trucks until all were packed full.

On 20 August, five days after the evacuation of Fresnes prison, British and American forces entered and liberated Paris.

A total of 2453 men, women and some children were evacuated to Germany on this final train. Apart from the airmen, only 300 would ever live to see France again.

★   ★   ★

It was the dogdays of August. Even before the doors were slid shut and padlocked conditions in the unlit, overcrowded cattle trucks were unbearable, with the sun beating down relentlessly on the black roof half a metre above the heads of the occupants. Conditions worsened once they were closed in, as the interior temperature rose and the air became stuffy and fetid.

A drag of heavy barbed wire was arranged behind the train to deter any escaper planning to break loose and lie down between the tracks while the train was moving slowly. Every fifth waggon was a guards' van, each one equipped with a wooden observation box.

The French Red Cross had managed to distribute a little food and some cigarettes to a few of the prisoners, but their supplies did not go far amongst the crowded and hungry multitude. Little did the prisoners realise that the cattle trucks would be their homes for the next five days, or that the many discomforts they would endure were merely a prelude to the greater hells of the concentration camps in Germany.

As part of the growing passive resistance to German occupation the French railway network had gone on strike, and it was only after a delay of several hours that the Germans came up with a locomotive capable of drawing the crowded train away from Paris.

Time dragged by, and the prisoners perspired freely in the stuffiness, cursing the Third Reich while trying to get comfortable. Some could sit down, but the majority had to remain standing. In every car agreements were reached as to how many could sit down at any one time, and the rest time they would be permitted before another group took their places. Nobody talked much about the coming night or their prospects of sleep. Finally a steam whistle sounded down the line, followed moments later by a sudden clang and lurch as the engine mated with the train.

After ten minutes' activity the train jerked, couplings rattled and the train began to surge forward. The overladen convoy of cattle trucks wormed its way out of the freight yards a little before midnight. Although it was only moving slowly, some fresh air began to flow into the carriages through the four small ventilator windows which had been laced with barbed wire. Everyone ate a portion of their food, although no water

67

was permitted: it was strictly rationed in each van and those who protested their thirst were shouted down by their fellow travellers. The train rumbled on into the night, although it would stop jerkily from time to time before resuming the nightmare journey.

Men and women alike, many suffering terribly from dysentery, had to endure the degradation of performing their toilet functions in the middle of the crowded boxcars. The stench, compounded by a lack of substantial ventilation, was appalling. As each toilet pail filled it began to slop about in the dark interior, and the clothes of those unlucky enough to be crammed nearby were saturated by the foul wastes.

The train trundled slowly on that night, heading due east towards the city of Nancy. Sleep was virtually impossible for the occupants, most of whom eventually dozed while standing, rocking back and forth supported by those around them. Several tried lying down, but there was insufficient room. Many harsh words were spoken as people tried to protect what little space they had, but in time everyone became resigned to the fact that he or she was going to suffer equally, and a grim silence prevailed.

Realising that they were moving further away from the scene of possible freedom, some of the men in Tommy Blackham's car began prising three boards from a half-rotted wall of their cattle truck. At three o'clock they were still hard at work when the train stopped unexpectedly. Shots rang out further down the train as a squad of guards moved towards them, searching for any signs of escape activity. When they saw the damage to the wall of Blackham's car the men were ordered out and made to strip naked while the damage was repaired. They were then directed back into the cattle truck, their clothes returned, and a general warning issued that if so much as a hand was seen outside any truck, the train would be stopped and hand grenades tossed through the door of the offending truck. When the train moved on again, the guards would fire a volley of shots every so often to demonstrate their vigilance and to serve as a warning.

At dawn, the train was attacked and strafed by an Allied fighter. Fortunately there were no injuries and little damage on this occasion, though there were subsequent attacks and the added dread of strafing or bombardment made the prisoners' lot even more unendurable. The airmen knew well that any trains moving across France by day presented fat targets to the swarms of fighters and bombers from England.

Later that morning, having travelled 70 kilometres from Paris, the train hauled into a long tunnel at Nanteuil-Saacy where it screeched to a halt. Outside the unlit cattle trucks the Germans began shouting and there was a lot of loud activity. Beyond the tunnel lay a rail bridge over the shallow river Marne, but both the bridge and the exit to the tunnel had been destroyed by Resistance operatives making a last-ditch effort to halt the train.

The exhausted prisoners suffered for a while in resigned silence, but as the locomotive continued to belch pungent smoke in the blocked tunnel, a new problem arose as the smoke found its way into the darkened boxcars. Panic set in as the occupants began to cough and choke on the thick fumes. Packed into trucks towards the rear of the train, the airmen and the women were comparatively fortunate. But the hordes crammed into the leading boxcars began to beat the walls and cry out into the darkness. As the noise swelled, the Germans, who also found conditions in the tunnel quite untenable, shouted back even louder and fired shots through the upper walls of the closed trucks.

After much shouting and panicky jostling, the frightened occupants were finally relieved to feel the train slowly shunting backwards out of the tunnel. Later estimates of the time spent in the suffocating blackness vary from one to three hours, but the darkness, heat and fumes made each minute an eternity of fear and uncertainty. Several men and women had fainted standing up.

Eventually the doors on all the cars were opened and the prisoners informed that the train could go no further. Their initial excitement was dashed when it was explained that they would be transferred to another train located in a tunnel on the other side of the river. Originally positioned at a siding near Nanteuil-sur-Marne, this train had been emptied of its cattle to make way for the evacuees. The prisoners were further informed that it would be necessary for some of them to carry all items of baggage, the guards' packs, and other stores across the remains of the bridge to the other train.

One truckload of men was detailed to this task, with six of their number kept under guard as hostages. Everyone in the detail was warned that escape attempts would result in the six men being shot. The occupants of an adjoining car were ordered to cross over to the waiting train and load the baggage and freight as it arrived. The remaining trucks were then locked up once again.

Later in the day the male prisoners were permitted to relieve themselves on the embankment by the train, followed soon after by the women, who were forced to line up facing the train in full view of the guards and the men moving the equipment. Bob Mills, who made four crossings of the damaged bridge, recalls averting his eyes from this humiliating spectacle. The Germans allowed each waggon to empty its toilet pail—the only time this would be permitted throughout the journey—and to refill the water pails. Les Whellum and French-Canadian Leo Grenon volunteered their services as water carriers, and were able to drink their fill from the river as they replenished each of the pails.

Throughout the afternoon the work detail made repeated crossings of the Marne. When their work was done the remainder of the prisoners were ordered out of their trucks in staggered batches and marched down the embankment to the fields beside the track. Here they were told through interpreters that they would have to take a detour of about six kilometres, as the Marne had to be crossed by a bridge at the village of Tiernay further downstream. The officer in charge ordered that several of the guards' packs and some other stores be carried by the prisoners, and reminded them that hostages were being held.

As the exhausted prisoners moved out of the culvert they encountered a fresh threat—a muscled SS guard who began lashing out indiscriminately with a long, thick baton. The men had to pass by this brute as hurriedly as possible, but few avoided the stinging blows he handed out. Phil Lamason was horrified at the sight of this bully beating his men, especially when he saw a young Englishman, Philip Hemmens, hanging back from the screaming German. Hemmens had a broken arm which had received only cursory treatment and binding. Without hesitation, Lamason strode over to Hemmens, grasped him by his good arm and walked him out of the column. He took the young man up to one of the senior guards, who was watching the proceedings with obvious uninterest.

'You must tell that guard to stop beating my men!' Lamason demanded. 'We are prisoners of war, and cannot be beaten by rotten bastards like him!' He pointed a shaking finger towards the culprit. The German surprised Lamason by speaking good English. 'You are not prisoners of war,' he stated firmly. 'You are terrorfliegers—child murderers. No, you are not prisoners of war.' Nevertheless he cast a look at Hemmens' arm. 'This man is injured?'

'Yes, dammit!' Lamason replied.

'Then I will have a word with my colleague,' the German promised. 'But every man, no exceptions, must help us to move. Perhaps your man can carry some straw for the compartment floors?'

Lamason looked at Hemmens, who exhaled with relief and nodded. The German strolled over to the red-faced guard and spoke to him in a stern but muted tone. The man scowled but lowered his baton. Malcolm Cullen remembers the temporarily uplifting detour that followed:

> The journey was slow but made a pleasant change after the night in the truck. At least we could breathe fresh air again. The road led through a village and the people were very sympathetic and showed contempt for our guards at every chance they got. They threw us bread and fruit and some of our boys managed to get a drink of cider. Water pumps along the roadside were besieged and the guards had to become threatening to move the boys on. After making about five or six kilometres in the shape of a horseshoe, first down the river and across, then back up the other bank, we came to a place opposite the tunnel where the hill sloped down straight into the river. In the cutting a line of cattle trucks were backed down to the bridge approaches and stood awaiting passengers. Into this train we went and the doors were again locked.

Canadian Art Kinnis recalls that it was not long before the airmen began sizing up escape opportunities from their new train:

> We were all repacked into the all-too-familiar boxcars, some of the chaps finding as many as 90 aircrew and French civilians in one car. We were lucky, for our car still contained 70. The French Red Cross were again on the spot and we got some sour milk, bread and coffee. Some of the cars were fortunate and received roasted potatoes. At this point one of the guards handed one of our chaps a hammer, telling him to fix the nails holding the barbed wire over the windows. With this object in his hand, and the previous knowledge that one of the floorboards was loose, it took but a quick bend and the board was made easily movable and ready for future use. The window nailing was completed to the guard's satisfaction and the tool was handed back. This was the start of an advantageous and disastrous time for that car.

The journey was soon resumed and, contrary to expectations, the train made good progress. That night followed the same pattern as their first, with many prisoners falling asleep on their feet and collapsing in exhaustion on top of their disgruntled companions. Two surprise stops were made while the guards checked the carriages with torches. Their diligence would be dramatically rewarded on the second inspection.

After their departure from the river Marne, and following some work on the floor of their carriage, a handful of men in Art Kinnis' cattle truck prized up the loose floorboard and the one next to it. They began slipping out while the train was travelling slowly up an incline, darting away from the tracks once their carriage had passed. Canadian Flying Officer Dave High of 419 Squadron, from Edmonton in Alberta, was followed into the night by six equally desperate Frenchmen. One of these men was spotted by a guard and shot down by a wildly spraying machine-gun as the train shuddered to a halt and pandemonium erupted. One squad was despatched to round up the escapees, while the rest of the guards stood watch along the tracks, ready for any further commotion.

The majority of the escapers, including Dave High, were rounded up and dragged back to the train. All the occupants of the damaged carriage were shoved to one end and counted. Their latrine pail was kicked over, potatoes and other food items squashed underfoot, and there was heated talk of shootings. Surprisingly, however, the Germans did not seem anxious to take any immediate reprisals. Once the offending boards had been nailed down securely the men were left alone, although Dave High did not entirely escape the wrath of his captors.

I was beaten with a rubber hose. I was struck mostly on the head, shoulders and arms, and was able to move about only with great difficulty for three or four days. I was black and blue for weeks.

As the train moved off the door of their boxcar was left open, and two guards stationed at the far end of the truck kept a close watch on the tightly-packed occupants. The men were still expecting some form of reprisal, and their fears increased a little after dawn when their train slowed and halted in the middle of the countryside. They heard the ominous crunch of approaching footsteps and then a Prussian officer, his face scarlet, addressed the prisoners through the open door. The Dutch pilot Spierenburg was one of the occupants, and he squeezed forward to translate. The officer roared at the Dutchman for the best part of a minute, during which time the pilot's face tightened and paled. Even those who did not understand German heard the word geschossen (shot) punctuating the tirade. When the German had finished he moved off and the Dutchman turned slowly to face the others, badly shaken.

'I've been instructed to tell you that to prevent further escapes, and by way of punishment, 35 RAF airmen and 20 Frenchmen from this carriage are to be shot!'

At this news a loud howl of protest went up, and the guards stiffened themselves for action. The prisoners selected to die were quickly separated from the rest and ordered from the truck, the Frenchmen cursing and shaking their fists at the Germans. Two machine-guns were set up on tripods a short distance from the carriage and the men were told to form three lines parallel to the train. Many of the airmen and most of the Frenchmen began to pray, and a muttered revolt swept through the intended victims. Word quickly spread that they would charge the Germans the moment a shot was fired. The first line of 20 men was ordered to step forward a few paces, and the machine-guns were trained on them. Les Whellum, in the front row, looked down the barrel of death and shivered.

I thought, this is it Les; goodbye to sweet life. I was staring straight down the business end of a machine-gun, and my Lord that hole looked huge. I can't remember whether I was frightened or just somehow resigned. It really comes as a dreadful shock when your enemy points a weapon at you, and you suddenly realise that your life might end right there and then.

Tense seconds passed, then a minute had gone by. The air was thick with emotion as the guards waited for the order to commence firing, and the men shook involuntarily with fear and anticipation. The officer in charge stood stock still. All was quiet, and to the men every second spent waiting for death was an agony.

Suddenly the German barked an order, at which the guards behind the machine-guns rose and stood to attention. The Dutchman was called over and the officer spoke to him briefly. With that he strode off, issuing orders to his men as he went.

The relieved Dutchman approached the group by the train. 'He's decided not to shoot you after all,' he said. 'He feels the lesson has been learned, but that the next escape will bring the most severe punishment.

He has ordered all of you to remove your clothes, together with everyone still in the carriage, and give them to the guards. They will be returned once we get into Germany.'

The men, still shaking, quickly divested themselves of their clothes, which were gathered up and removed. They had been fortunate, and knew they had come within an ace of being slaughtered. Their water pail was removed, the damaged floor repaired, and the door padlocked. Their nakedness now added to the men's misery, but they realised that further protests would not only prove futile but could provide the Germans with an excuse to shoot them.

That same day, 18 August, the train pulled up for another snap inspection. In the cattle truck from which the escape had taken place a fourteen-year-old French boy grasped the ledge of one of the small ventilation apertures, intending to pull himself up so he could see outside. He had either forgotten the order to keep his hands away from the window, or was just being foolhardy. As he hauled himself up to peep out, a guard watching for any such movement opened fire with his Schmeiser. One of his bullets hit the youth across the knuckles, shattering his hand. He fell to the floor, screaming as he clutched his bloodied hand against his chest.

Moments later the door of the boxcar was unlocked and flung open, and the guards demanded to know which of the naked occupants had disobeyed their orders. The youngster was easily spotted and a guard called him over. Canadian Harry Bastable, a first-aid man, demanded medical treatment for the boy, but his entreaties fell on deaf ears. The lad clambered unsteadily to his feet and moved over to the door, where he was grasped by the guards and flung out onto the ground. Several of the closest occupants were also ordered to get out.

The prisoners watching from the open boxcar, and those peering through knotholes and cracks in the other waggons, saw two grim-faced guards grasp the boy under the arms and haul him to his feet. They asked the tearful youth if he was French or English, and he stammered that he was French, following which he was motioned to proceed down the slight incline by the track. As he moved off a Feldwebel unclipped his Luger and shouted an order at the guards. They lifted their Schmeisers and fired at point blank range into the boy's back. The youngster threw his arms wide and then slumped forward, face down onto the ground. The Feldwebel walked down the

74

incline and stood over the prostrate form, aimed his Luger, and fired two bullets into the back of the boy's head.

The faces of the men watching were a study of incredulity; not a muscle moved as they stood in shock at what they had witnessed. The German calmly swung around and ordered two more men to come forward from the ranks. The guards grabbed the two closest, Leo Grenon and Englishman Dick Rowe, and the Feldwebel ordered them to bury the body. The naked men were given small field shovels with which they hacked out a shallow grave in the hard road ash of the embankment. Dragging the youth's body up to the grave, they buried him as best they could before they were ordered back, silent and grey-faced, to their cattle truck. They stopped briefly to wash their hands in a pool of water by the tracks, then rejoined their companions.

As the train pulled away from the scene the dead boy's hands and feet could be seen protruding grotesquely from his shallow grave. Several of the men felt ill. They too had touched the lacing of barbed wire over the small window, and had even emptied pails of excreta through it.

When the train finally passed through Luneville and Saarbrucken and moved into the Fatherland the tension felt by the guards eased noticeably. Although their vigilance did not relax on the infrequent stops they were visibly pleased to be away from French soil and the risk of attacks by the Resistance. The naked men had their clothes returned.

For two more days and nights, punctuated only by unsettling Allied strafing attacks and surprise searches by the guards, the train rolled on. The Germans need not have worried excessively about further escapes. The prisoners had grudgingly accepted that such attempts would only bring a swift and terrible retribution.

The occupants of the cattle trucks grew dirtier, more despondent and miserable with every passing kilometre. Every waggon stank of human waste, vomit and body odour. The prisoners itched and perspired incessantly, and were ravenously hungry and thirsty. Added to this, the burning need for sleep had sapped the last of their energy.

Rumours began to sweep the cattle trucks. The train seemed to be heading towards Frankfurt, and all aircrew knew that outside Frankfurt lay Dulag Luft—the Luftwaffe interrogation centre where captured air force prisoners were taken for questioning prior to their dispersement to proper POW camps. On the fourth day, the lookouts by the windows reported that the train was indeed approaching Frankfurt. Hopes rose but quickly faded as the long train roared into the main station and swept out the other side without stopping.

On the fifth morning the train slowed once again and a station signboard came into view. Word of their whereabouts quickly went around the cattle trucks—Weimar. The airmen held brief discussions as to their location, and it was decided that they were some 80 kilometres south-west of Leipzig.

The railway staff switched the rail tracks 100 metres behind the last carriage, then another locomotive backed out of a siding, linking up with what had been the last cattle truck. The five cars carrying the female prisoners were uncoupled and the locomotive moved off, taking the women to what would prove to be their final destination—the concentration camp at Ravensbruck. Once again the tracks were switched and the shortened train containing all the male prisoners began to back up. It made its way onto a side track and began to pick up speed. The prisoners felt they were now close to their destination. Finally the train braked and slowly came to a stop.

Outside, emaciated men dressed in filthy clothes were working beside the tracks. The Dutch pilot stood up to the window and started to question them in German. When he finally lowered himself the others were keen to know their location.

'It's a place called Buchenwald,' said Spierenburg. The men muttered amongst themselves—nobody had heard of the place.

'I'm afraid it's one of the worst concentration camps in Europe,' he continued. 'Not a prisoner of war camp, but a punishment camp. I rather fear we are all in big trouble.'

No one moved, no one spoke. Finally someone cleared his throat and uttered a heartfelt expletive.

A few shouts came from outside, then the train began to move once again. The clank of steel on steel seemed to break the spell, and the cattle trucks were soon alive with conversation. The French prisoners were visibly nervous, while the airmen were angry that they were not going to a Luftwaffe camp under the protection of the Geneva Convention. The engine crawled up a long incline then coasted downhill until it finally rolled into a temporary platform surrounded by barbed wire.

The doors were unlocked and rolled back, and the occupants were ordered to get out. If the prisoners thought their guards on the train had been harsh, they soon discovered that the SS guards from the camp were far worse. As the prisoners were dragged from the cattle trucks, those who fell to the ground were brutally kicked until they got up. Anyone slow to respond received a boot to the back or a punch in the face. Vicious dogs snapped at the men's bodies and tore at those on the ground.

Off the platform and assembled on the road known as the Caracho Way, they were moved along at double time, whipped and beaten to make them move faster. They finally reached a set of large iron gates in which the words 'Buchenwald Konzentrationlager' had been forged. The beatings continued as the men moved through the gates and into the camp. One American flight sergeant who had suffered a badly sprained ankle when landing by parachute had his walking stick kicked from under his arm as he passed through the gates. 'There are no cripples in here!' a German major growled.

Further along the road they passed the Kommandant's office and the Political Department where selected inmates would undergo Gestapo interrogation. The men finally passed through another iron gateway, which opened up beneath a large tower. On either side of this tower were brick wings lined with steel shutters, which they soon learned were the bunkers, or punishment cells. Next they entered into a large compound, where they were made to turn right and then halted outside a large brick building. All around the new arrivals were hundreds of men dressed in ragged striped garb, who sat or stood pensively watching them from a cobbled area. The new intake of prisoners was made to sit down in columns, taking the opportunity of this break to finish off any scraps of food they had been saving, as well as passing around a few precious cigarettes. The French even managed to produce some chocolate. The established inmates, kept at a distance by the guards, watched every move with craving in their eyes.

After a while the new arrivals were ordered to stand and wait in the scorching sun as the French prisoners were separated and ushered roughly into the brick block, having been told to remove and carry their clothing.

A pungent, sickly smell hung over the entire camp, drifting around with the thick smoke belching from a tall chimney atop a squat building on the far side of the barrack area. The men innocently assumed this building to be an incinerator, but all too soon they would come to know of its more evil function as the camp crematorium.

The official International Red Cross Excerpts from Documents, issued by the International Tracing Service at 3548 Arolsen, Germany, states that the 'Polgende Haftlinge' prisoners arrived at Buchenwald on 20 August 1944. The salient remark on this document is the acronym 'DIKAL [Darf in kein anderes Lager]'—Not to be transferred to another camp—an instruction that the airmen were never to leave Buchenwald. It is considered a blessing that none of the men was aware of this fact at the time.

The arrival date at Buchenwald is further authenticated by a document from the SS archives in the Buchenwald Museum. Dated 28 August 1944 and signed by the SS Haupsturmfuhrer, Camp Medical Officer, there is a complete breakdown by camp registration number of the entire intake of prisoners who 'arrived from Paris on the 20th August 1944 and were placed in the Zeltlager [tented camp, within the Little Camp]'.

Against the serial numbers 78266 to 78423 (some numbers were not allocated to the new arrivals) appears a heavy annotation: 'TERRORFLIEGER'.

4

Bloody, Bloody
Buchenwald

On 28 February 1933 Germany's new Reichschancellor Adolf Hitler
introduced the Presidential Emergency Decree, which allowed
for the 'protective custody' of political opponents to the Third Reich,
in order to safeguard and enlarge his new regime.

Heinrich Himmler, who had been appointed Reichsfuhrer of the
Schutzstaffeln (SS) in 1929, was installed into the position of Chief of
the German Police, and the decree gave him virtual *carte blanche* to set
his feared SS and Gestapo to the task of rounding up anyone they
deemed to be enemies of the state, including gypsies and Jews, who
were referred to in the decree as 'inferior races'.

Hitler and many of his followers harboured a manic hatred of the
Jewish people, as evidenced in Point Four of the Nazi Party program,
which declared: 'Only a member of the race can be a citizen. A member
of the race can only be one who is of German blood, without
consideration of creed. Consequently, no Jew can be a member of the
race.' This volatile doctrine was preached across Germany virtually from
the moment Hitler took power, and was used by the Nazis as a means of
implementing their master-race policy. First the German people were
encouraged to boycott any Jewish enterprise, and then a series of laws
were passed which effectively displaced Jews from every department of
public administration. They were ejected from the civil and armed services,
and forbidden to hold posts in higher professions such as education.
Soon Jews were no longer permitted to own businesses or make purchases
in gentile stores, and were prohibited from marrying gentiles.

A single Jewish grandparent was sufficient ancestry to qualify as a
member of this so-called 'inferior race'. Brilliant Jewish academic Albert

Einstein was ousted from his position as Director of the Kaiser Wilhelm Physical Institute of Berlin, following which he sailed to America, while Sigmund Freud was forced to flee Vienna in 1938 for exile in Hampstead, England. He died of cancer the following year.

Germany's Jews were not arrested as a matter of general policy in the formative years of the Nazi regime, but many were picked up by the Gestapo on vague and often spurious charges and finally sent to work in the concentration camps, where they were treated as vermin. Tens of thousands of ordinary citizens were thrown into these camps, from where there was very little chance of return.

Gypsies were being similarly rounded up before the war, and placed in the camps as part of the Nazi campaign against those they referred to as shirkers and asocials. Previously they had simply been moved on, but Himmler prohibited the customary wanderings of these nomadic people, and their encampments became subject to constant raids and arrests. Himmler reasoned it was better to get rid of this 'scum', as he called them, by sending them to the work camps. In 1942, orders were promulgated which stated that any gypsies remaining in Germany, irrespective of age or sex, were to be sent to the camp at Auschwitz for extermination. With very few exceptions, Germany's gypsy population perished within the confines of Auschwitz or other concentration camps.

The Gestapo and SS worked in collusion: the Gestapo rounded up the prisoners, while the Allgemeine department of the SS was designated the responsibility for staffing the camps.

Buchenwald concentration camp, which later became the first large extermination camp to be seized intact by Allied advance troops, was eight kilometres to the north-east of the historic and cultural city of Weimar, capital of Thuringen, and was built on the lower slopes of the fog-shrouded Ettersburg—a mountain rising 700 metres above sea level.

The camp was one of three first planned by the SS Totenkopfverbande (Death Head Unit) for permanent sites as early as 1936, and ultimately operated for eight years. The other main camps were located at Dachau, near Munich, and Sachsenhausen, near Berlin-Orianienburg. Dachau was located in southern Germany, Sashshenhausen the north, and Buchenwald the central region. As with later camps such as Ravensbruck, Auschwitz and Belsen-Bergen, they were administered from Berlin. By the time Hitler invaded Poland in 1939 there were six camps in operation, containing 20 000 inmates. Soon there would be nearly a hundred, as the shadow of Nazi domination swept across Europe.

Prewar, the massive influx of dissidents, political prisoners and 'undesirables' meant that the new camps had to be built quickly, but forced labour was easily obtainable. And so to the work-site at Buchenwald went the Jews, gypsies, Jehovah's Witnesses, homosexuals and the feeble-minded. The devastating Holocaust, with its promise of 'racial purity', had begun.

The site for Buchenwald camp was a former estate, bequeathed to the SS by its allegiant owner, and covered 140 hectares of rugged and well-wooded, previously uninhabitable beech and pine forest. The camp was opened on 15 July 1937 as KZ (Konzentrationlager) Ettersburg, but less than two weeks later the name was changed to the less austere Buchenwald. On 27 July more than a thousand concentration camp inmates, mostly convicts and political prisoners, began arriving under escort from the established camps of Dachau and Sashsenhausen to commence the mammoth, back-breaking task of clearing the woodland slopes. Standartenfuhrer Karl Koch of the SS was appointed by Himmler as the first Kommandant of Buchenwald, and he brought with him his new wife, Ilse, who would achieve a notoriety far exceeding that of her husband.

The prisoners were forced to work fourteen hours a day under the most primitive of conditions, and with very few tools. They were subjected to continual torment by their guards, who kicked and beat them with little compunction. Guards who shot down any prisoners, ostensibly on the flimsiest excuse of an escape attempt, were actually rewarded with additional pay, promotion and leave passes. Labour was easy to come by, and fear made the prisoners work without pause, in the terrible knowledge that even the slightest hint of flagging or rebellion was keenly looked for, and even manufactured, by the guards.

Parties of workers were taken to the nearby stone quarry, where they were subjected to further harassment from their foremen—generally convicts who had elected to work in this post for extra rations. These foremen would sometimes snatch a cap from one of the prisoners, toss it away and order the unfortunate man to run and pick it up—at which a sentry would shoot the man for making an 'attempted escape'. The sentry and foreman would later share the bounty. If the sentries decided that work in the quarry was progressing too slowly, they would roll or throw huge rocks onto the terrified workers below them. Those not fast or lucky enough to evade the rocks suffered fearful injuries or death.

Water for the workers was scarce during the autumn of 1937, and sanitary provisions consisted of two massive open pits, each eight metres long by four metres wide and deep. Over these lay several indescribably fouled logs, on which squatted as many as fifteen dysentery-stricken men at any one time. One hideous and common sport practised by the guards was to rush the toilet area without warning to see how many prisoners would fall in panic from their precarious perch. Those who fell tried to scramble to the earthen banks of the pits but many, too weak to extract themselves, died in the thick excrement, the laughter of their tormenters the last sounds they heard. To go to their aid involved the risk of sharing their fate.

In clearing the terrain of trees and vegetation, many of the massive tree roots were painfully and unnecessarily dug out by hand. The SS guards did not issue any digging implements, preferring to watch the prisoners clawing at the hard earth with their hands. However, one massive oak, known widely in the area as Goethe's tree, was spared the fate of the lesser pines around it. According to local legend the revered poet had once meditated beneath its branches, so German officials not only spared the tree, but planned that it would eventually dominate the centre of the new camp. It seemed to take on even more imposing proportions as the ground around it was cleared and exposed.

In fact Goethe's tree was seemingly so indestructible that the inmates quietly developed an improbable superstition concerning it. When the tree fell, they declared, so too would Hitler's Third Reich. The expectation that this would occur was impossibly remote. Incredibly, however, the tree did actually fall towards the end of the war without the hand of man touching it, and in death it became an embodiment of hope and freedom to those who witnessed its destruction.

But the site workers in 1937 were indifferent to the future of Goethe's tree as they slaved on into the terrible winter months, when temperatures on the newly-exposed slopes would sink as low as -22°C. As planned, the SS quarters were finished first, so Germany's soldiers could spend their evenings in comfort while the prisoners slept in wretched, inadequate shelters.

Farcical rollcalls were held, during which the prisoners stood for hours on end in the freezing cold. Every prisoner, living or dead, feverish or badly beaten, had to be present, the only exceptions being hospitalised inmates or those on detached work details. The roll call on 28 October 1937, with the temperature at -15°C, lasted 18 hours and 20 minutes, and was drawn out until the Germans were happy that the tally of living and dead was correct. The following year, during evening rollcall on 14 December 1938, the count was down by two and the lightly clad prisoners were forced to stand for 19 hours through a bitterly-cold night. By morning 25 men had frozen to death. When the prisoners were finally dismissed at midday the number of dead had risen to 70.

On occasions the guards would search prisoners at rollcall. All pockets had to be emptied and the contents examined. This was generally an excuse for the guards to confiscate any money or tobacco they found, but at times they carried out full strip searches simply as an act of humiliation. The prisoners were compelled to stand completely naked for several hours, during which time Ilse Koch and the wives of some SS officers would often inspect the prisoners through the wire fence of the compound, pointing out different men, laughing and making lewd comments.

A number of prisoners attempted to escape, but generally these were futile bids, and the mandatory penalty was death. In the spring of 1938 a gypsy was recaptured after making an unsuccessful break for freedom and Kommandant Koch decided to use the man to set an example. He was shoved into a wooden box so small the man could only crouch, and the open side of the box was covered with chicken wire. It was then placed in a prominent position in the rollcall area. Under Koch's orders several long nails were driven into the sides, back and top of the box, which meant that the man was unable to change his cramped position without piercing his flesh. For two days and three nights the gypsy's agonised screams rent the air. On the third day he was given an injection of poison to put an end to his suffering.

On 15 June 1938 a group of around 500 Jewish prisoners arrived at Buchenwald. Following the standard delousing process these men were consigned to a sparse blockhouse commonly known to the inmates as 'the sheepshed'. They were worked to the limit of their physical endurance, existing on a pint of thin soup and a loaf of bread to be divided amongst five men every day. Many times even these rations were stolen and sold by the barracks orderlies. The Jews began dying of exhaustion and maltreatment, with pernicious abuse a daily ordeal. Within eight weeks 150 of these men had died or taken their own lives, while the rest were physically incapable of continuing the strenuous work. Then a fresh intake of 2200 Jewish workers, mostly Austrians, arrived from Dachau.

The November 1938 assassination by a Jew of German Embassy Secretary vom Rath in Paris by a Jew resulted in a massive retaliatory round-up of Jews across Germany. A further 9800 Jewish workers were sent to assist in the construction of the camp at Buchenwald.

By 1939 over 40 hectares had been clawed bare and building was well under way. A typhus epidemic caused the camp to be quarantined for a time in February, but work went on. Only a small part of the site was actually allocated to hold the planned 20 000 male inmates—the greater area had been set aside for the lower SS ranks and for an impressive headquarters building. Apart from the extensive administration building and barracks were such incongruous showpieces as carefully tended zoological and botanical gardens, a game preserve, falconry court, a cinema, and even a riding academy.

Dr Eugen Kogon from Munich, a political prisoner held for several years at Buchenwald, described some of the animals kept at the zoo as 'five monkeys and four bears...even a rhinoceros'. One of the more sadistic pleasures of Kommandant Koch was to have prisoners locked in the bear cage, where they were ripped apart by the savage beasts. Over the years much of the food allocated to the camp as prisoner rations was diverted to the zoo's animals.

By the beginning of the Second World War the concentration camp was fully functional. Proudly mounted above the main gate to the camp was the Buchenwald motto, 'Recht oder unrecht—mein Vaterland', literally 'My Country—right or wrong'. An electrically charged fence nearly four kilometres long surrounded the prisoners' enclosure.

Entrance to the main camp compound was made through an iron gate set within a narrow gatehouse, which was straddled by a two-storey brick and wooden guardhouse, surmounted in turn by a searchlight and clock tower. Fashioned into the gate was yet another slogan, 'Jedem das Seine' (To each his own). On either side of the gatehouse were steel-doored punishment cells known to the inmates as bunkers, and beyond it lay the main rollcall or Appell area, a dusty rock-hard compound which was transformed into a cloying quagmire when the rains came. The wooden huts beyond the compound were roughly constructed and earthen-floored, without windows or sanitary facilities. The inmates were still forced to use the rough open pit toilets.

The camp itself was set out in two sections—the Main Camp, with its brick buildings and wooden huts, and the Little Camp, in which conditions were indescribably wretched. Here the excess of prisoners were bunked in horse stables, originally intended to house twenty-eight beasts, but which were soon crowded with up to 2000 men at any one time. Squashed together, three or four men sharing a single thin blanket, and generally in putrid wet clothing, these exhausted and undernourished men slept on tiered wooden bunks. Washing facilities were primitive, personal hygiene was practically non-existent, and epidemics regularly coursed through these barracks.

Prior to the completion of a permanent crematory at Buchenwald in 1941, a mobile unit was installed in order to dispose of those who had died. The combustion chamber in this crematory was quite small, and the bodies literally had to be crammed in. Sometimes smaller body parts were not completely cremated, and these gruesome remains were often scattered across the rollcall compound.

From October 1942 the shipment of Jewish prisoners to the death camps for annihilation became mandatory, and this policy remained in force until the summer of 1943. By then a severe lack of manpower resources meant that the surviving Jews found themselves being used as slave labourers rather than being fed into the gas chambers and later cremated. Spared the immediate threat of extermination, they were worked at a gruelling schedule to the point of physical exhaustion.

The camp perimeter at Buchenwald was constantly patrolled, while machine-guns protruded from the guard towers, or miradors. At night, searchlights illuminated the electrified wire.

A five-kilometre asphalt road named Eicke Street (after the chief of the SS Death-Head unit) meandered away from the camp and was bordered by elite SS residences. It finally led to a cluster of luxuriously appointed villas belonging to the Kommandant and his senior officers, who delighted in the centrally heated comforts while enjoying sweeping views over the magnificent Thuringian Plains from the sheltered southerly slope of the Ettersburg. In a well-guarded stockade enclosure beyond the road stood the isolation huts, specially constructed as barracks for politically prominent inmates.

The Kommandant's wife Ilse Koch made special use of the riding academy hall at Buchenwald. This massive construction was nearly 100 metres long and 40 wide, with mirrored walls and a roof suspended more than 20 metres above the bark-chip ring. Frau Koch made frequent morning rides in the hall to the musical accompaniment of her own SS band. A former bar girl, the plump, red-haired and nymphomaniacal Ilse had accompanied her husband to the concentration camp in 1937, where she quickly became known to the inmates as 'The Bitch of Buchenwald'. With good reason they feared her more than their sadistic guards.

Ilse was born in Dresden in 1907 and by the age of fifteen was working in a cigarette factory. Although never a great beauty, her glorious red hair and energetic sexual appetite attracted many young men to her bed, where she allowed them to indulge their fantasies and aberrations on her willing body. She later worked as a bar girl and then as an assistant for an elderly bookseller, whose business thrived due to his under-the-counter sales of pornographic literature. One of the book store's best customers was a conceited young Gestapo officer by the name of Karl Koch.

Karl and Ilse quickly became lovers but both had strong sexual appetites and by mutual consent they actively pursued different bed partners. Ilse set about seducing most of the bedazzled young officers from his regiment, giving a bemused Karl her rating of each as a sex partner. When Himmler promoted Koch to colonel and appointed him Kommandant of Buchenwald it came with a strong recommendation that he should marry, and make his wife chatelaine of the camp. Karl and Ilse, with an eye to the future, quickly complied.

The power of her non-accountable position soon turned Ilse into one of the most feared and sadistic creatures of the war. Accounts given at her postwar trial testified to her debauchery while at Buchenwald, and made for horrifying testimony, yet every incident was verified by witnesses eager to see justice brought to bear on this despised woman.

On many occasions she would ride her horse through the prisoners' compound wearing nothing more than a brief swimsuit. The object of this exercise was to feign outrage if any inmate dared give her so much as a sideways glance, or to look for anyone whose sight displeased her. The penalty for such trivialities was a severe whipping or beating. On one such occasion an unfortunate inmate was caught furtively peering at her. On Ilse's orders the man was held face-down in a muddy puddle until he drowned. Another time she was seen to take up a pistol and participate in a cold-blooded massacre of over 20 prisoners. She would order teams of terrified inmates to run around the compound dragging heavily-laden carts, singing at the tops of their voices, and gave the name 'singing horses' to this activity.

Ilse's appetite for sexual perversion grew with her unchallenged power over life and death. Several times she was known to select a suitable prisoner for a night's orgy in company with her husband, whose bisexuality added to Ilse's enjoyment. In the morning the prisoner was taken away and executed lest he reveal any details of the night's activities. During her husband's five-year tenure at Buchenwald Ilsa gave birth to two sons and would often frolic in the nude with them on the lawn of their luxurious villa.

Eventually Ilse's carnal excesses even grew too much for her husband, who found more sedate pleasures sodomising young boys from the compound. But Ilse's perversions continued unchecked and soon a horrible rumour began to spread around the camp that she was killing inmates and using their skin to make gloves. Later evidence not only proved these rumours to be true, but far worse was to come.

At the time of the liberation of Buchenwald a gruesome display of items was put together for photographs, later to be used in evidence at Ilse's trial. According to witnesses she would ride around the compound seeking out prisoners with attractive tattoos. She would have any such victim seized and taken to the camp dispensary, where he was killed by means of a poisonous injection. The skin bearing the tattoo would then be carefully removed, cleaned, and tan-dried in the camp's pathology department. The resultant tattooed strips were then manufactured into lampshades and other household 'ornaments'. One man's tattoo which took Ilsa Koch's fancy bore the words 'Hansel and Gretel', while a favourite table lamp—a birthday present for Ilse—was manufactured from human bones with a shade made of skin.

An important witness at Ilse's postwar trial was a worker from the pathology department, Joseph Akerman. He told of seeing hundreds of skins being stripped from the bodies of murdered inmates on her specific orders, and even recalled the birthday lamp. 'It was a complete lamp made of human skin and bone,' he testified. 'The light was switched on by pressure against the little toe of one of the three human feet which formed the stand.'

While Frau Koch used the camp and its inmates as her playthings, her husband began to grow wealthy by utilising the camp's labour force to his own advantage. Despite Himmler's doctrines of so-called honour and integrity within the SS, Karl Koch amassed a quick and considerable fortune by sending camp labour out to local private concerns who willingly lined his pockets in exchange for a cheap, expendable work force. However, Koch's greed proved his undoing when he came under the suspicious eye of local tax authorities who claimed that huge sums of money, around a million marks in all, had been misappropriated by the Kommandant.

SS leader Prince Waldeck, the supreme legal authority in the district, brought the matter to the attention of Himmler, who refused to believe that such unsubstantiated charges could be laid against a trusted officer of the SS. However, in February 1942, while the charges of corruption were being investigated by the SS, Koch was transferred and given the position of Kommandant at a smaller concentration camp in Lublin. Here he once again began to use his influence to line his own pockets, but his past began to catch up with him. Several months later SS investigators at Buchenwald uncovered overwhelming evidence of his crimes and this, combined with the testimony of informants, caused him to be arrested.

Himmler was said to be furious at his officer's betrayal and demanded an example be made of him. Koch was tried by an SS tribunal, found guilty of profiteering, and given the option of death by firing squad or serving on the Russian Front. However, Prince Waldeck would have none of that. Mindful of Himmler's outrage he overruled the judgment of the tribunal. Karl Koch was taken back to Buchenwald where, looking out over the scene of his crimes, he was summarily executed by firing squad just days before the camp's liberation in April 1945.

With her husband's transfer to Lublin in February 1942 Ilse Koch remained at Buchenwald, albeit in the reduced position of a domestic staff member under the new Kommandant, SS Colonel Hermann Pister. Frau Koch, her formerly unquestionable authority now greatly diminished, was to remain at the camp with her children for another two years.

At the Buchenwald trials, convened at Dachau on 14 August 1947, 22 Nazi officials of Buchenwald concentration camp were sentenced to hang by an American war crimes court. Ilse Koch, aged 41 and eight months pregnant, was among those who received a life sentence. During the trial she repeatedly denied any of the charges against her, to the clamorous hoots of derision from those assembled within the court. She then resorted to a pretence of being mentally unbalanced, but this made no impression on the judges. A plea for clemency due to her imminent motherhood was put forward but this was also rejected. The pregnancy, which occurred while she was in prison awaiting trial was never officially explained. After the birth her baby daughter, whom Ilse would never see again, was sent off to a Bavarian orphanage.

On 17 October 1949 the Americans struck a deal with the Bavarian Minister of Justice and 'released' Frau Koch. She was immediately rearrested by the Germans and tried for incitement to murder. On 15 January 1951 the German courts found her guilty and she received her second life sentence.

Still holding hopes of eventual release from Aichach prison Ilsa began learning English and took to writing poetry. She corresponded with some poor misguided soul in Australia who had written to her in prison and even spoke of emigrating there to marry him on her release. But her lawyer's efforts to secure her release were all in vain. On 1 September 1967 Ilse Koch tied a strip of her bedsheet around her neck and hanged herself from the cell door.

* * *

Ilse Koch was not the only person to take advantage of unlimited power over a helpless and wretched assemblage of humanity. Killings were commonplace at Buchenwald, and the methods employed were mostly barbarous.

By 1942 block number 46 had been constructed for use as a medical experiment centre. Here prisoners were used as human guineapigs in a variety of sinister studies, which included injecting them with typhus and experiments on how long a man could survive on a diet of sea water. Unskilled and discredited practitioners worked at discovering vaccines for a vast array of diseases including smallpox and cholera. They freely indulged themselves in the practice of unnecessary surgical techniques attempting to cure, among other 'anti-social' diseases, homosexuality.

Decompression and cold water survival tests also saw many of the victims to an early death. Men were immersed in freezing water for varying times then placed between two prostitutes from the camp brothel. If they survived, the recovery time was noted. Inmates destined for the crematorium ovens were sent via the experimental block where they received injections of phenol, milk, or sometimes just air. At the Nuremberg Trials in 1946 Eugen Kogon gave the following testimony:

> In Block 50 I saw photographs of phosphor burns taken at Block 46. One need not be a specialist to imagine the suffering of people whose flesh was burnt down to the bones. When the experiment was completed after three months, all those who survived were liquidated.

Kogon, who served as a medical clerk at Buchenwald, also spoke of a fearful torture perpetrated on some poor unfortunates.

> Dreaded even worse than whipping was the punishment that involved being trussed up against a tree. Like all other penalties, it was imposed in entirely arbitrary fashion. It was executed in the following way: the hands were tightly tied on the back and then the body was hoisted up by them and suspended some six feet high from a tree or post, the feet hanging free and the entire weight resting on the twisted shoulder joints. The result was extremely painful shoulder dislocations. The victims screamed and moaned frightfully. Often they received beatings on face, feet or sexual organs to boot. The helpless sufferers cried for water, for their wives and children, for a bullet to end their torment. Those who lost consciousness were revived by being drenched with cold water. This punishment lasted from half an hour to four hours. Those who survived it almost invariably sustained permanent injuries.

The camp's crematorium and mortuary block was a single-storey building with a basement below ground level. A stone staircase led down into the dank basement—the last steep steps for many prisoners. Those not escorted down the steps were simply shoved through a trapdoor in the floor above.

Embedded in the stone walls of the basement were 48 open steel hooks, set about two and a half metres above the floor. The doomed prisoners would be tied back to back, and loose nooses made of piano wire placed around their necks. Then, in pairs, they were hoisted up until the nooses dropped over the hooks and then they were allowed to hang. It was a cruel death. One unnamed former inmate, who looked into the basement after the liberation of the camp, recalls seeing scratch marks low down on the stone walls, where the men had frantically kicked out in their brief death throes. After five minutes had elapsed the bodies were lifted down. A 'coup de grace' was then administered by means of a heavy wooden club, crushing the men's skulls. The bodies were then despatched in a large electric lift to the ground-floor crematorium, which had the capacity for disposing of almost 400 bodies a day.

To corrupt the more powerful of their political prisoners the SS even established a brothel at Buchenwald, bringing in girls from another death camp at Ravensbruck who had been falsely promised they would be discharged after six month's 'service'. After serving their time the girls were simply shipped back to Ravensbruck and a fresh consignment sent in. The SS hoped that the senior inmates at Buchenwald would be more responsive to their commands if they were given the luxury of spending 20 minutes at a time with some of the women. However all this really did was cause a further corruption of power within the camp hierarchy, with the more feared German Communists exerting their power over their subordinates in order to obtain extra gifts for the women, which in turn gave them lengthier sojourns in their beds. The majority of the camp's senior men avoided the brothel and its temptations. Higher-ranking members of the SS also took advantage of the brothel, and they could be found behind its doors at all hours of the evening.

Thousands of Buchenwald prisoners were used as forced labour in Germany's war factories, built underground to protect them from Allied air attacks. Assignment to these armament factories was a virtual death sentence; the Germans could never relinquish a prisoner who had been engaged in such secret work, and once they had outlived their productive usefulness they were killed. Some natural caves within the Kohnstein mountain near Nordhausen were converted into an underground concentration camp, a Buchenwald subsidiary known as Dora. During the later war years prisoners at Dora were forced to live in filthy conditions and work 12-hour shifts on the production of Hitler's V-weapons. They would not see daylight for weeks on end.

Dozens of louse-infested, emaciated corpses were transported from Dora to the Buchenwald crematorium every second day, and the mortality rate never fell below 1500 per month. These emaciated bodies were intertwined in death, and the first gruesome task on arrival at Buchenwald was to wrench each louse-infested body from the filthy pile of corpses.

Two armaments factories operated on the outskirts of the prisoners' compound at Buchenwald, obviously positioned to deter area bombing by the Allies. The Gustloff Armaments Works was a factory funded by appropriated Jewish funds and property seized by the Nazis' regional leader in Thuringa. The Deutsche Ausrustungswerke (DAW) was a general armaments and radio factory owned by the SS, under trusteeship of the camp Kommandant Hermann Pister, which turned over an annual profit of half a million marks to Himmler's war coffers.

The prisoners who worked in the Gustloff and DAW factories not only took to acts of sabotage, but succeeded in smuggling out weapons such as rifles and hand grenades. These arms went to a secret military resistance group within the camp, and were eventually used in the successful uprising which saw the camp liberated.

Prisoners arriving at Buchenwald were designated a camp number, and it was by this number they were identified and answerable from that time on. After passing through the Effektenkammer (effects store— these days the camp museum) they were stripped of all their money and possessions prior to undergoing removal of all their body hair and showering in an adjoining block. All of these new arrivals were then placed in the Little Camp quarantine area awaiting work orders from outside armaments factories. They were then subjected to a cursory medical examination, following which they were graded for duties according to their physical fitness levels. Their next move was into the Main Camp, where the Arbeitstatistik raised a personal working card for each prisoner and allocated them to specially constituted working parties, known as Kommandos. These Kommandos were still functioning when the group of airmen arrived at Buchenwald in August 1944, and former KLB prisoner Stanley Booker explains what would befall the unfortunate inmates on the work details:

These Kommandos, known as Transports, gave cause to the greatest terror and apprehension, for they were used solely to dispose of inmates on expendable working parties. The Transports left the camp daily, marched out behind a magnificent military band in circus-type uniforms of gold lace and red velvet, which had originated in an Hungarian State Opera. After a varying period as slave labourers in the various outcamps and factories, the telling twelve-hour working days resulted in the prisoners becoming exhausted and burned out. At this stage they were returned to the Main Camp for extermination in the camp crematorium.

Within the camp itself, those inmates fortunate enough not to be allocated to external working Transports were detailed off daily to various internal tasks, such as the dreaded quarry or camp sewage pit, ditch digging, railway and road maintenance, camp administration, kitchen details or miscellaneous duties in the medical block.

The actual camp itself was divided into two components—the Main Camp which comprised the prewar accommodation surrounding the main Appell Platz (rollcall compound), and the Little Camp, used as the quarantine area. It was accepted that conditions in the Little Camp were exceptionally bad, and that any long-term prisoners kept there and not allocated to an outside Kommando within the first few days were considered expendable. One of the most feared Kommandos was to be detailed to work in the camp quarry, located on the extremity of the Little Camp, from where most of the labour was obtained. This was where the greatest number of deaths were recorded every day. The prisoners were forced to break stones with the most basic of tools, load them with their bare hands into rail tipper trucks, and push them up a steep incline to the surface level. Inmates were liquidated by being driven to sheer exhaustion, and that's when they were shot by the guards or simply beaten to death.

Another of the unsavoury characters inhabiting the camp in the early war years was the notorious hangman of Buchenwald, SS Scharfuhrer (Master Sergeant) Martin Sommer, whose dominion was the isolation cells or bunker, located in one wing of the gatehouse. The bunker comprised a series of compact concrete cells, each with a small window embrasure and radiator high on the wall, and a raised concrete platform which served as a bed. A magnifying peephole was set into each door so the prisoners could be monitored, and any transgression, however minor, was rewarded with 25 lashes of the whip.

The bunker was used for the interrogation and torture of prisoners, and Sommer was adept at both. One of his favourite methods of interrogation was to have the prisoner stripped naked and then alternately immerse his victim's testicles in ice-cold and boiling water. After a while the skin would begin to strip from the man's scrotum, at which Sommer would splash on a 'treatment' of iodine, causing the prisoner excruciating pain.

According to evidence given by him during the trial of Kommandant Koch, Sommer was personally responsible for the torture and death of over 150 prisoners in one six-month period. He flogged, stamped on, hanged or deliberately poisoned any prisoner brought to the bunker. As a confidant of the Kommandant, even the SS at Buchenwald feared Sommer and they soon became aware that he held sufficient power to have any of them transferred or even eliminated if they displeased him.

On arrival at the bunker each prisoner was stripped and searched, then tied to the radiator in his cell to await the attention of Sommer. Should the prisoner be found asleep during this time he was thrashed mercilessly by a guard. The killings were administered in a variety of ways. Sometimes Sommer would simply hang the man from the window or radiator of his cell; at other times he would beat them to death with an iron bar. In one instance he placed a prisoner's head in an iron clamp, which he screwed tight until the man's skull was crushed.

There were many verified examples of his barbarism. In one instance, in 1940, seven Jews were being held in a single cell when Sommer entered carrying a tin water pail. He proceeded to beat two of the men to death with the pail, following which he tore a piece of iron from the radiator and in a frenzy of unbridled rage used it to kill the other occupants.

In his 1950 book, *The Theory and Practice of Hell*, former prisoner Eugen Kogon relates many of the inhumanities practised by Scharfuhrer Sommer during his reign of terror in Buchenwald's bunker.

It was . . . customary to feed the prisoners cathartics in their food, until they fell sick with bloody stools. Of course there were no antidotes. There were two toilets in the bunker, one for the prisoners, the other for the SS. Whenever a prisoner received his 25 lashes, he had to bend over and immerse his head into the excrement-filled toilet bowl. When the punishment had been administered, he was not permitted to wipe the excrement from his face.

On one occasion Sommer shackled seven young Polish prisoners to their cots. Their diet was reduced to salt water and pickles, until they perished. Bunker orderly Gritz describes how their fearful screams, and finally moans, pierced his eardrums.

Some of the tortures inflicted by Sommer were nightmares of sadism. He liked to strangle prisoners with his bare hands. His greatest sport was to herd all his prisoners into the corridor, about four feet wide, where he had them do kneebends and hop about until they dropped from exhaustion. He would then trample them with his heels, until the blood spurted from ears and nose and at least a few were left dead. On one occasion he crowded fifteen prisoners into a single cell, giving them only a children's chamber pot which they were not permitted to empty for some ten days. The floor of the cell was ankle-deep in excrement. Subsequently Sommer murdered all fifteen men.

His own quarters were decorated with an illuminated skull. At night he would sometimes summon a victim from one of the cells and leisurely do away with him in the room. He would then place the body under his bed and fall asleep peacefully, his work well done.

Such was the place to which the airmen arrived on 20 August 1944. By that time such evil protagonists as Sommer and Kommandant Karl Koch had been removed from power by Himmler, and the influence of Ilsa Koch was greatly diluted. However, the industry of mass extermination continued, and by late 1944 physical conditions had deteriorated even further as the numbers of prisoners increased due to Hitler's unchecked policy of eliminating those he regarded as subhuman.

According to the official statistics, a total of 238 980 prisoners were admitted to Buchenwald between July 1937 and March 1945, of whom 56 545 died. Approximately 161 000 prisoners left the camp for work at armaments or munitions factories, or were transferred to other death camps.

* * *

For several hours after their arrival at Buchenwald the airmen stood under the heat of the afternoon sun. However they were more were concerned for the safety of the French prisoners who had shared their nightmare train journey across France and Germany. On arrival at the camp these men and boys had been forced to enter a large brick hut, and they had not emerged.

As the airmen waited for something to happen, Phil Lamason walked up and down, instructing the men that they were to conduct themselves as a military body, and would accordingly march correctly whenever they were moving about the camp. He reiterated that they were rightfully prisoners of war, and not political or criminal prisoners. Military decorum was to be maintained at all times and the orders of superior officers obeyed, come what may, until representation could be made through the proper channels. His words encouraged the men, who respected the stocky New Zealand squadron leader, and they bore their circumstances with markedly more dignity. Nevertheless, as Tommy Blackham recalled, it was difficult for the airmen to maintain their discipline and silence at times:

Every time an SS man came along we had to stand to attention and take our hats off. All our personal belongings had been confiscated—these included military identity discs which, the Germans said, could be bought in France for a few francs.

When it came time for the airmen to strip and enter the brick building Lamason directed the Dutch translator Spierenburg to object to this treatment on behalf of his men, claiming the rights of prisoners of war. These appeals were ignored and the first of the men were shoved into an ante-room in the building. Here, any remaining contents of their pockets were placed in an envelope while all their clothing was checked into a bag which was then tagged with their names. A Canadian airman, Ed Carter-Edwards, vividly remembers their following painful welcome to Buchenwald:

They cut off all our hair, every strand from every part of our bodies. The guys who sheared us were Russian prisoners from the camp, which at that time held around 40 000 people. There were Russians, Poles, Czechs, French, every nationality imaginable; political prisoners, soldiers, black-market agents, and everything else. The fellows who clipped us were most unkind. They used old-style clippers, cutting underneath our arms and between our legs. They were so rough they nicked us pretty badly; we were bleeding all over, and to finish off their pleasure they used a swab and stuck it in a pail of fluid and dipped it under our arms and between our legs. It was some kind of lye and oh, did it burn! Imagine nearly 170 airmen dancing around like stripped chickens. It was funny but painful at the same time.

Totally devoid of hair and clothing the men were told they had to have showers and were ushered into a large adjoining shower block. They entered with great trepidation, for the word had gone around that the Germans frequently killed prisoners by placing them into a so-called shower room, which was in reality a gas chamber.

Buchenwald was one of several Nazi concentration camps that did not have gas chambers and the men's relief when sprays of steaming hot water spluttered out of the ceiling fixtures was profound. After their shower they were issued half-metre square rags, each of which was to be used as a towel by two men. Having dried themselves as best they could they were moved on and into a clothing store. Here they were issued with their prison garb of cotton shirt, trousers and a cap—all of

Flight Sergeants Eric Johnston (left) and Jim Gwilliam.

Flying Officer Kevin Light, DFM.

Flight Sergeant Mervyn Fairclough.

Flight Lieutenant Malcolm Cullen.   Flight Lieutenant Les Whellum.

The cafe in Coivrel where Jim Gwilliam and Keith Mills hid out in a small upstairs room.

Above: Fresnes prison, on the outskirts of Paris.

Right: The prison's interior, showing the unusual layout and narrow walkways between the cells.

Rollcalls at Buchenwald required daily counts of thousands of prisoners in the area known as the Appell Platz.

The dreaded quarry, where life was cheap and the workload brutal.
(Photos: Buchenwald Memorial Museum)

which had seen better days, and were hand-me-downs from previous inmates. Prior to their reissue the clothes had been baked at high temperatures to kill off any lice lurking in the seams. No shoes were issued and the men had to go barefoot.

Once dressed, the airmen were taken back through the gateway to a large office for registration, where a battery of scriveners—prisoners like themselves, but wearing black armbands and berets—ordered them to give personal details for their camp registration forms. These forms required information the airmen were not prepared to reveal, so they only gave their name, rank and service number. Stratton Appleman from the USAAF recalls that events surrounding this mass obstinacy contained a little serendipity.

After a lot of pushing and shoving, it soon became apparent that we were expected to form into a single line for moving through still another building. Apparently I was the first military person in line, and because all communication was in German or French, I had no idea of what was going on. Once I got toward the head of the line, however, I thought it was just another interrogation.

An elderly gentleman addressed a question at me, first in German, then French, then Spanish. When I responded 'I am an American Air Corps officer; I speak English only and I demand recognition as a prisoner of war', the interrogator asked in English, 'What part of Texas are you from?'. He explained that like most of the other authorities in the camp other than those in uniform, he was also a prisoner. In fact he had been a political detainee for some twelve years following a career in the German consular service. His language skills had caused him to get the chore of interviewing prisoners for assignments, either in the armaments plant at Buchenwald or on work details elsewhere. Despite the fact that I had inadvertently confirmed his guess about my geographic origins, I told him that I must follow my military orders to furnish only my name, rank and serial number. After a half-hearted attempt to convince me that he wanted only information pertaining to my personal skills and abilities—absolutely no military information— he conferred with his colleagues then asked me to step aside.

I felt once again that my adherence to military orders had paid off. Seeing a few Americans I recognised in the line behind me, I explained what had happened and urged them to pass it on. As each of the downed airmen reached the interrogator, they explained their status and asked for POW status. Each was asked to step aside.

Thus we created a bureaucratic problem for the camp authorities which had the effect of uniting us. It was only then we got a comprehensive picture of how many of us were in the same predicament, and it was only then that we came to be dealt with as an entity.

This mass defiance by the airmen soon attracted the attention of the foremen prisoners, known in concentration camps as Kapos. They threatened the airmen and banged their fists on the desks, but to no effect. In the face of this small storm of rebellion, the senior Kapo finally ordered his clerks to take the minimum details available and issue each man with a small white cloth tag bearing his prison number. He was furious, but kept himself in check. The men were then individually photographed, holding a slate on which had been chalked their five-figure camp number. They felt they had won a small victory as they assembled outside the office in the heavy night air, but their smiles faded when they were surrounded by a squad of SS guards armed with lumps of wood. The Germans began shouting, and clubbed into the group of prisoners, urging them to run back through the gateway along the stony road. Heavy blows rained down on them as they ran and staggered barefoot along the path and through the gate, finally assembling with the French prisoners once again in the parade area under the watchful eyes of the guards.

Following another count they were lined up in columns of five and marched toward the wired-off area known as the 'Kleine Lager' or Little Camp, an already-overcrowded space for new arrivals. As they gingerly marched to the Little Camp, other prisoners lined the bordering wire fence to ask the men their nationalities. When these inmates realised that many of the new arrivals were Anglo-American they were both surprised and elated. In a multitude of tongues they pleaded for news of the war from the passing airmen in a multitude of tongues. Frenchmen wept, and cried out to their countrymen that the war would soon end. For some of the British airmen it was a surprise to hear an occasional shout in English; they later learned they came from a few Channel Islander dissenters, imprisoned after the Germans occupied the Islands in July 1940.

The prisoners trudged on past row upon row of dark green wooden huts of one or two storeys. They turned a corner and moved down a small incline, at the foot of which they were counted through a gate, and then again at another gate 100 metres on. Barbed wire surrounded them at all times. By now it was nine o'clock, and darkness had closed in as they entered the Little Camp.

As the final gate closed behind the new arrivals they looked around their cobblestoned pen in dismay. It held no building other than a small stone construction five by three metres in size housing the Lager Altester (Camp Senior) and his assistants, and the only form of cover apart from two large trees was provided by five crowded marquee-style tents, which housed only the very sick.

Their position was quite evident—they would have to sleep out in the open. Some blankets had been issued to the exhausted men, but not enough for all. Nevertheless, they cleared the area and made themselves as comfortable as possible before stretching out on the cold, hard cobblestones to sleep. Surprisingly, an urn of lukewarm soup was delivered to the new arrivals and was soon consumed using some communal bowls and spoons. For many it was their first meal since leaving Fresnes.

The following morning at 4 a.m. the prisoners in the Little Camp were roused for rollcall, a slow and tedious process after which a third of a litre of cold ersatz 'coffee'—a bitter brew actually made from acorns— was issued to each prisoner. The newest inmates of the Little Camp were then free to wander about, talk to each other and get the lie of the land.

There were almost 3000 people in this section of the camp, including Russians, Poles, Jews and Frenchmen—some of whom were known to the prisoners. Phil Lamason recognised his former helper Georges Prevost, and managed to talk to the distraught man at length. Prevost had shed a lot of weight.

The brick building they had noticed the previous night housed a latrine at one end, which was in constant use, while in a room at the far end the bodies of those who had died during the night had been stacked for transportation to the camp crematorium. Jim Hastin recalls peering through the window one day and counting seventeen corpses.

In the rectangular area between the tents and the stone hut was a large cobbled mound known as the Rock Pile, and this was to become the airmen's quarters. Elsewhere, the ground was a clay-like black soil. Through other prisoners they soon came to know something of the organisation of the camp.

Each block had its block-fuehrer or Altester, all of whom were long-term political or criminal prisoners who had succumbed to treachery with the promise of extra food rations, other privileges, and less work. These masters among the underlings were placed in a position of authority over the prisoners of all nationalities.

The regular prisoners' garb was the standard blue and grey striped pyjama-style clothing, while the Germans in authority wore black berets and armbands lettered 'Kapo', 'Lagerschutz' or 'Vorarbeiter'.

Each prisoner category wore a different coloured triangle on their jacket and trousers to denote their race, allegiance or crime, with an individual serial number on a white cloth patch below the triangle. In the case of 'other nationalities', a black letter indicating their origin was embroidered on a red triangle. F stood for French, T for Czechs, R for Russians, P for Poles and so on. The colours of the triangles indicated the class of prisoners as follows:

Red without letters — German political prisoners
Red with black letters — Other nationalities
Green — Common law offenders
Yellow — Jews
Pink — Homosexuals
Violet — Jehovah's Witnesses or others imprisoned for religious beliefs
Black — Gypsies, 'shiftless elements', and work dodgers

A parade or appell was held every evening, when prisoners were meticulously counted, first by the block-fuehrers and then by SS guards. Appell for the main camp was held on the large compound, where a floating population of prisoners, numbering in their tens of thousands, were counted. If German guards needed to be addressed at these rollcalls, it had to be from a distance of at least three metres.

Working parties were marched out of the camp every day after the 4 a.m. appell in all types of conditions. The majority of these prisoners would either hew stones in the quarry, drag logs, or work on roads or other nearby utilities.

Food consisted of a small daily ration of the tough black knackerbrod, a third of a litre of soup, and coffee. The ersatz coffee was always cold by the time it was delivered at the Little Camp. If so much as a drop was spilt or splashed out of the urn the entire carrying detail was beaten by the guards. The soup and bread also came in urns, and were issued at eleven o'clock. The so-called 'soup' was little more than grass or nettles soaked in hot water, often containing bugs and maggots and sometimes a cube or two of meat from an unspecified source; the unleavened black bread was topped by a cursory wipe of margarine substitute.

The airmen were appalled at the sight of the other prisoners fighting and scratching to scrape the bottoms of the food urns once the issue had been handed out. The strong beat the weak underfoot, and the weak sometimes died. But survival was the grim game, and those who have never known the desperation of true starvation could have no appreciation of the effect it can have on otherwise rational human beings.

Apart from the soup they'd been given on arrival, the first food the airmen received were small individual portions of dark grey bread, which smelt vile and tasted even worse. Several men unthinkingly threw it away in disgust, and were amazed at the ensuing panic as literally dozens of starving inmates rushed at it, fighting for the pathetic scraps like wild beasts, scratching, punching and elbowing each other. With a mixture of pity and disgust the other airmen tossed their bread into the rapidly growing melee. The following day they tossed their bread ration to a group who had patiently waited nearby, but this practice was quickly brought to an end by Lamason. He did not want his men to be responsible for any deaths or injuries. Furthermore, he reminded them that the bread was their chief source of sustenance, as there was little nourishment to be had in the evil-smelling soup, which was merely used to soften the bread somewhat. This meagre meal was washed down with their half-cup ration of lukewarm coffee.

Dysentery was rife in the camp, so the men began toasting their bread over small fires, hoping that by burning it the resultant carbon might prevent or alleviate the disease.

As Senior Officer, Lamason soon chose seventeen officers to help him maintain discipline amongst the men. Each of these officers then became responsible for his own unit of nine or ten men. This served not only to better organise soup and food distribution, but enabled the leaders to know at least a few men reasonably quickly. One of the first assignments Lamason gave these leaders was to mount a guard detail both day and night to prevent pilfering by other prisoners, which had begun their first night in the Little Camp.

Buchenwald was an extremely big camp and most nationalities were represented in the prisoner population. There was considerable political friction amongst the prisoners, although by this time an International Camp Committee had been formed to prepare a united front against the SS. As the airmen would soon come to learn, the most powerful of the factions were the German and French Communists, Polish and Russian nationalists and Czechoslavakians.

Early on in the life of the camp the anti-Fascist prisoners found that the best way to protect and assert their interests was to place their own men in positions of importance. Later, when the SS tried to displace these power-holders with their own men, the outsiders found themselves without any effectual authority due to the organisational structure already in place, and were soon withdrawn. Eventually the SS came to realise that better discipline was achieved within the camp if the prisoners were permitted to organise and administer the camp routine. There were no further attempts to counter the hemegony set up by the political inmates at Buchenwald. According to former political prisoner Eugen Kogon, the German Communists brought the best qualifications to the accomplishment of this task.

> In contrast to men of liberal views, they had always been inured to absolute party discipline, and in methods and means they were almost the only ones who were the enemy's match. In addition they had the most extensive camp experience. It is to be regretted—and was actually the cause of certain setbacks—that especially in the early years the Communists excluded anti-Fascists of persuasions other than their own, but in practice it could not be helped.
>
> Within their own ranks the Communists were by no means unanimous, though they suppressed dissent with an iron hand, occasionally even by the murder of dissenters. Distrustful of anyone not of like mind, they were out to support only unconditional followers of the prevailing Communist party line. Only occasionally did they come to accept selective collaboration with others.
>
> The positive achievement of the Communists on behalf of the concentration-camp prisoners can hardly be overrated. In many cases the whole camp literally owed them its life, even though their motives seldom sprang from pure altruism but rather from the collective instinct for self-preservation in which the whole camp joined because of its positive results.

In the last year of the war, self-government by the inmates in Buchenwald was so inculcated into the day-to-day activities of the camp that the SS had no real idea of the internal situation—nor did they really care. They were exhausted by the years of bitter warfare and the realisation that defeat had become increasingly inevitable, so as long as the camps still ran to expectations they were happy to allow the Communists to mostly have their way in its administration.

This virtual abrogation of camp authority by the SS allowed the Communists to secretly organise a common front of all prisoners prepared to fight against their captors, and resistance activities were created both within and outside of the camp. Inmates employed in the camp office and the labour statistics department falsified information so that unskilled workers were transported to factories requiring highly skilled personnel, and they were able to preclude the sick and weak from assignment to hard labour details. Others helped sabotage the German war effort by ensuring that materials destined for armaments factories went astray or were the wrong type, technical drawings were subtly altered, and valuable resources were wrongly stored or wasted. Elsewhere, inmates working as doctors or medical attendants protected fellow prisoners slated for execution by altering their names to those of others already deceased.

As they came to meet and know prisoners of other nationalities in the Little Camp, so the airmen became aware of the horrors perpetrated at Buchenwald. They also learned basic but valuable survival techniques, such as boiling water when making a 'brew' to prevent the onset of dysentery. This water was obtained from the latrine building at certain hours of the day, and though attempts were made to keep the water pure it still stank even after boiling.

Due to their unique situation, and because of the non-transfer DIKAL endorsement on their papers, the camp administrators chose not to allocate any of the airmen to outside Kommandos, even though the SS doctor had passed all of them as fit for work. They knew the airmen were in Buchenwald illegally and could not be presented with an opportunity to escape. No one beyond the camp perimeter could ever know they were there. For the airmen, this at least meant they were assigned to such simple domestic duties as cleaning, carrying, and interior road maintenance.

Although the five tents served as hospitals, no place of healing was ever filthier, and it was common to see corpses being removed daily by the stretcher bearers. Other prisoners would momentarily stop to doff their caps or place a hand over their hearts as a mark of respect as a body was carried by. Everyday life then resumed. In these 'hospitals' paper bandages were used many times over on gaping, putrid wounds. No medicines were available, apart from the occasional aspirin. Medical personnel would pass from one patient to another, cutting decaying matter from open sores without any form of anaesthetic, using the same, unsterilised pocketknives.

Even standing at attention on appell was no guarantee of being left alone by the guards. On the airmen's second day, during the evening count, Bob Mills was standing at the front of the ranks in the accustomed air force manner—hands tightly clenched, thumbs pointing along where the seams of his trousers would normally be. Suddenly an SS guard roared up, yelling at the top of his voice and indicating a problem with Mills' hands, but the airman did not understand what he was doing wrong. The guard swiped his Luger across Mills' face, drawing blood, then strode off yelling and waving his gun. Bob Mills was later told that prisoners were required to stand with their hands flat by their sides to indicate they were not holding anything in them. The same thing happened to Ron Leverington from Hampshire the following day. Malcolm Cullen recalls that the men came to know their 'lager altester' (block senior) Hoffman quite well at appells.

He was a long term prisoner and was as mad as a hatter. He carried with him a heavy stick and had no compunction whatever in using it. It was common to be held to attention for three hours waiting to be counted, and if there had to be a recount the hours dragged on almost indefinitely. The madman rounded up all with the aid of voice and stick, and strode up and down in front of the ranks, with eyes blazing and jaws champing. His mouth never seemed to be still and he drooled horribly. Dysentery was common among those who had been in the lager for some time, and if these poor unfortunates were caught in the aborts [toilets] during appell they were chased and beaten unmercifully until their crazy overlord was out of breath.

Our group toed the line very strictly and seemed to impress this monstrosity by its military bearing and ability to understand and comply promptly to orders given by its Senior Officer. Apart from roaring at us frequently he did not trouble us very much.

5

Terror From the Skies

The morning of 24 August 1944 a special appell was called on the concrete area in the Little Camp. The 'terrorflieger' contingent were separated and each man was given two very painful injections of a green fluid in the chest. Being aware of the potential significance of some injections through prisoners working in the medical block, this was not a very happy parade.

However, at 11.45 a.m. the prisoners looked expectantly into the sky as the camp's air-raid sirens wailed out their warning, and the dull thudding sounds of bombing in the direction of Leipzig filled their hearts with some satisfaction. Vapour trails crossed the clear sky as most of the Main Camp inmates were rapidly shunted into their barracks. Many of the Allied prisoners elected to remain outside, watching with mounting trepidation as two large formations of Flying Fortress bombers from the US Army Air Force swept in—129 in all—and headed straight for the camp. Despite their understandable anxiety, the men were gladdened by the sight of so many aircraft flying in undisturbed formation over enemy territory.

Suddenly a Very pistol was fired from a window of the leading aircraft, and a white bombing marker hurtled to the ground—the signal to commence an attack. 'Jesus Christ—look out!' one of the airmen yelled. At the same time the terrified SS guards barked orders for everyone to lie flat on the ground, then covered them with machine guns, all the time eyeing the skies with apprehension. The targets of the American bombers this day were the Gustloff and DAW factories outside the camp, where the essential gyro components for Hitler's V-1 buzz bombs were being assembled.

105

The men heard the first bombs, a high whining sigh that grew and culminated in a series of earth-shaking explosions. The bombs landed a little over 200 metres from the prone airmen, who watched and felt the explosions with mixed feelings, and not a little admiration for the accuracy of the bombing as the nearby factories were destroyed, bomb after bomb exploding within their walls.

Streams of terrified workers began pouring out of the factories, but as they fled from one death so they ran headlong into another, as outraged guards shot them down in their scores. Political prisoners, Russian slaves and Jewish children alike were torn apart by the machine-gun fire and fell in heaps outside the blazing factories. The explosives within these buildings began to detonate, compounding the fearful destruction.

Very few bombs actually landed within the concentration camp itself. The bomb aimers above had used exemplary skill in destroying their targets, for the main part scrupulously avoiding the populated camp area. However, there was panic and chaos within the Main Camp. Incendiary bombs had started fires in several blocks, and the Germans were screaming panic-stricken orders, trying to direct the berserk hordes of prisoners. A group of 37 Allied secret agents being held in Buchenwald, who had remained outside their Block 17 quarters, cheered and hurrahed as the bombs wrought the destruction of the hated factories.

Several of the airmen sustained minor injuries, but none was seriously hurt by the shrapnel which flew in all directions, although Frank Salt would later have a small chunk of steel extracted from his back.

When the mighty Fortresses wheeled for home the last two aircraft, coming in low, dropped canisters directly over the camp. The prisoners ran in fresh terror as small detonations rent the bomb casings one hundred metres above them, but they released a fluttering cascade of white leaflets which floated slowly to the ground. Some of the more excitable European inmates rushed into the compound to pick up the leaflets and were shot by the trigger-happy guards. A batch of the papers rained down on the airmen, who eagerly plucked them from the air.

The leaflets displayed two small photographs, showing groups of uniformed Germans. The wording, printed in bold Gothic type, declared that 'These men are German prisoners of war in England. They are treated according to the rules of the Geneva Convention.' The leaflets caused quite a buzz. They indicated that the airmen's presence in

Buchenwald might already be known, possibly through Underground sources, and a warning had been served on their captors. Speculation was certainly rife. However, their relief was short-lived, as some armed guards rushed up shouting 'Alle Americanner und Englander—Aus!' Many of the men thought they were going to be shot, but the guards ordered them through the gates into the Main Camp, where they were instructed to begin clearing away the debris and to fight the numerous fires. Some of them were made to carry supplies from the blazing food store. While loathe to assist, the men though it prudent to comply, as the guards were quite jittery and seemed ready to open fire at the slightest sign of rebellion.

Barefoot and dressed only in trousers, the men began to beat out several of the smaller fires and clear some of the wood and brick rubble. Numerous unexploded incendiaries lay amongst the debris. The guards, standing at a cautious distance, ordered these removed as well.

It was hot, dirty and dangerous work, and the men sustained many painful blisters to their feet and bodies as cinders fell all around. Eventually the incendiaries had been cleared from the vicinity and bucket brigades had quenched the worst of the fires.

Several of the airmen assigned to moving food and clothing stores were able to purloin welcome supplies, but some went a little overboard. Phil Lamason, to his horror, came across one of his men wearing a highly polished pair of boots he had yanked off a dead German guard.

'You bloody fool!' he hissed. 'Get those off and get rid of them before another guard shoots you on the spot!' The frightened man quickly discarded the offending footwear.

Meanwhile the dead and injured were taken away on stretchers and planks of wood. Blackened, rigid corpses were strewn everywhere in and around the blazing huts, and the stench of burning flesh—a smell now well known to those within the camp—hung heavily in the air. In the centre of the camp many of the longer term inmates stared in amazement at the sight which confronted them: Goethe's tree had been hit by an explosive incendiary and was now just a blackened, shattered corpse. The despised symbol of the Third Reich's strength and supremacy had fallen.

In the Gustloff armaments works seven of the ten main workshops were totally destroyed, the boiler house was gutted, and other smaller buildings damaged. Within the garage and storage areas fourteen buildings were destroyed, nine severely damaged, and a large number of trucks blown to pieces. In the DAW enclosure thirteen buildings had been blown apart and another two gutted by fire. Gestapo headquarters had also been devastated in the raid, with eleven buildings flattened and set alight.

Seven buildings in the concentration camp were destroyed. In all, 175 1000-pound bombs had been dropped during the raid, as well as 583 500-pound bombs and 279 500-pound incendiaries—a total of 303 tons of explosives.

When the final death tally came to be known, it was revealed that nearly 80 Germans had been killed and around 300 wounded. The toll amongst the prisoners was appreciably higher, with almost 2000 casualties, including 400 dead.

*   *   *

Frank Salt, who had been hit and wounded by flying shrapnel, was taken to the Main Camp hospital for treatment. Art Kinnis later recorded his aircrew colleague's impressions in his diary.

> Karl, second in charge of the Little Camp, rushed him away to hospital. Out on the main road past the cinema they came to grips with a stream of wounded and dying prisoners, all on their way for what scant attention might be obtained. Once inside the hospital grounds it became apparent that the situation was far beyond control. Wounded were standing, sitting and lying everywhere. Hospital attendants were making crude attempts to aid the seriously injured, but if a man appeared well-bandaged he received no further treatment.
>
> Utter chaos was the scene that would greet everyone. Wounded were being carried on stretchers, planks, doors, in fact any object that would serve, in a continuous moving body to join this milling, suffering mass of humanity.
>
> Cases requiring operations were rapidly put to one side, but it was readily seen that the few doctors could not cope. Many were those that died on the lawns. They were stripped, roughly slung onto carts, and then hauled away when the load was sufficient for the human horses to pull. Efforts for comfort were few, medical supplies were quickly used up, but the suffering went on and on. Late afternoon coffee was served which, in its small way, was a blessing. The ambulance vans from Weimar arrived with medical supplies and were away in a flash for more urgent material.

The doctors by this time had sorted all into the serious and not serious, the latter (Salt included) being sent back to their barracks. Legless, armless, and badly mauled were still on the ground when Frank left, thankful to leave what will always remain a horrible afternoon.

One of those seriously injured in the raid was Princess Mafalda, the daughter of the King and Queen of Italy. The isolation barracks where she was held had been hit and gutted by fire, and she received severe wounds to her legs. As there was no women's hospital within the camp she was taken on a stretcher to the brothel where, held in the comforting arms of a weeping, distraught girl, she lapsed into a coma. Doctor Schiedlansky, the camp Medical Officer, was summoned to tend the Princess. Immediately on seeing her shattered legs he commenced a double amputation. The princess, clutched tightly in the girl's embrace, moaned and gripped her arms as the operation began, but the severe trauma and loss of blood proved too much, and she quickly succumbed. Her body was tossed on top of a heap of twisted corpses and later burnt.

The Germans were furious at the damage caused to the camp, and to their beloved Goethe's tree. Many of the guards screamed and spat at the airmen, calling them 'Verdammt terrorfliegers!' over and over.

That same day they were ordered to report en masse to the SS headquarters where, amid the devastation, Kommandant Pister took the opportunity to vent his personal hostility on the airmen. Parading up and down in front of the charcoal-covered men he gave them a tormented lecture through an equally excited interpreter on bombing and destruction and then, shaking his clenched and gloved fists, said he expected them to pay the cost of the damage! At this many of the men relaxed enough to actually smile, but the situation was too volatile to make any comment.

At the end of his tirade Pister's attitude suddenly softened. 'I am grateful for your cooperation in helping to clear the damage this morning. Your position here is under review.' The airmen were amazed. This was the first positive statement they'd had on their situation since arriving at the camp.

Later a German officer told some of the men that the SS had called upon their services to help clear up because they knew the airmen's integrity under pressure could be relied on, and it was known they would keep their heads under adverse conditions. They were further informed the SS had anticipated that such a raid on the camp might break the electrical circuit in the fence. Accordingly the perimeter was surrounded by guards armed with flame throwers, under orders to deal swiftly with any mass break-out.

*　*　*

Disease, in particular dysentery, began to strike at the airmen. The long appells became a torment of pain and shame, as they were not permitted to go to the toilets. To make matters worse, the sky paled to a watery grey, and billows of cumulus cloud began piling up in the west. If the rains came, as seemed inevitable, the men feared the worst.

Some days after the bombing raid the sky turned black and a slight drizzle began to fall. Thunder rumbled in the distance as the men's blankets slowly became soaked, while the cobbles on which they lay grew wet and slippery. The rain stopped mid-morning, but the sky was still overcast and the wind had risen to a stiff breeze. Then the skies opened up and the rain belted down.

For the next two days the men fought against the elements until, when it seemed they would all die from exposure, they were moved to a wooden barracks block in the next compound up the hill. As they marched up in driving rain with blankets over their heads, some took off their shirts and tried to keep them dry by holding them under their arms. Finally they made their way into the crowded block and found places for themselves on the floor.

Block 58 was a windowless hut 30 metres long and eight metres wide. There were no bunks, but four tiers of wooden shelves divided into compartments in which three men had to sleep under conditions barely suitable for one. In fact they were more like wide bookcases than beds. These shelves were packed with sleeping bodies when the airmen arrived, amongst them 500 German gypsy boys, aged from six to sixteen. There was no room for the newcomers, but they were grateful that they now had a roof over their heads. They wrapped themselves in their damp blankets and dropped off to sleep.

The rain continued for several days and the airmen seldom left the barracks except for the compulsory appells, although the work continued as usual for the other prisoners. There was much to be horrified about in their new quarters, but the new inmates were especially appalled at the age of some of the gypsy children in Block 58. In talking to other prisoners they discovered that a special block had been set up in the main camp specifically for children other than the gypsies.

110

This children's barracks, in Block 8, was crammed at that time with nearly 2000 youngsters from a variety of countries. Almost all were of Jewish extraction, children of executed partisans and Soviet and state officials. They had been wrenched from their parents' arms for transportation to Buchenwald, and most would eventually go to other camps such as Auschwitz, where their lives ended in the gas chambers. The first children arrived in Buchenwald in 1939, together with the Polish prisoners, and were given chores within the grounds such as cleaning officers' barracks and helping in the kitchens.

A group of anti-Fascists had demanded that the children be accommodated in their own block and the SS camp administrator had reluctantly agreed. This solidarity amongst the adult prisoners protected the children against some of the more brutal treatment by the SS. The inmates were even able to set up an education system using the talents of Soviet and German teachers, in particular a gentile Czech who not only taught the children but was appointed to supervise their barracks. These anti-Fascist prisoners fought their hardest battles in trying to keep the children in Buchenwald when they were scheduled for transportation and ultimate liquidation. Through their efforts a total of 904 children were able to survive the war.

The youngest child ever to inhabit Block 8, registered on arrival as a 'partisan', was just four years old! His name was Stefan Jerzcy Zweig, and the struggle of the prisoners for his young life was later described in Bruno Aptiz' evocative novel *Naked Among Wolves*.

There were 765 prisoners crowded into Block 58 with the airmen, and at night the air became exceedingly foul. The French, Jewish and gypsy inhabitants were running with lice, which swarmed all over the newcomers and nearly drove them mad. By this time, 35 of the airmen were considered ill enough to be detained in the camp hospital.

A few days after they moved into Block 58, a group of gypsies was evacuated to another camp—and probably the gas chambers—leaving only 450 in the block, which meant that the airmen were able to find space in the shelf-like beds around the walls. Life became slightly more tolerable for them, despite the fury of the lice and fleas. Each man had only about 45 centimetres of sleeping space, with no mattresses or pillows, and only one thin blanket between three or four, but it was certainly better than sleeping outside in the rain.

They were not permitted to write home, and there were no Red

Cross parcels. The barrack lights went out at 10 p.m. and the area was patrolled by SS guards with ferocious dogs. Sport or recreation of any kind was forbidden. The various nationalities gave the airmen some camp money, known as lagermarks, and with this they were allowed to buy cigarettes from the canteen building at a rate of 25 per man per week.

In one corner of the hut stood a large earthenware washtub, where the men were able to wash their faces and hands but little else, and they were forced to use their own shirts as towels. There was a small, filthy toilet block positioned just outside their barracks. Inside, this consisted of a trench just over a metre wide, which tapered down to a third of that width a metre and a half below. The sides and bottom of the trench were concreted, and some constantly-running water carried most of the effluent away. Along each side of the trench was a single rail, supported at intervals by sturdier, rough-sawn rails over the trench. The men, most suffering the effects of dysentery and dizzy from disease and a lack of nutrition, were forced to squat on these bridging rails. A little further away was the main latrine block, built in a similar fashion but on a larger scale.

The Frenchmen in Block 58 were forced to work outside of the camp during the day, mostly in the quarry, returning exhausted late in the evening. Sometimes they managed to bring back some garlic with them, which they shared around. It was carefully cut up and placed onto stale slices of bread, which helped to make these a little more palatable. On odd occasions their watery soup contained suspicious shards of meat which the men devoured stoically.

Every morning a handcart pulled by prisoners from the Little Camp did the rounds, and the bodies of those who had died during the night were piled on top. In the final months of Buchenwald's operation there was a critical shortage of coal, and bodies waiting to be cremated were thrown onto piles situated all over the camp. Rats swarmed through these piles, greatly increasing the threat of a typhus epidemic, and something had to be done. Permission was finally received from Himmler to conduct mass burials, but this interment in vast graves was generally confined to German prisoners; even in death it was not appropriate to bury Germans and Jews in the same grave.

On one occasion Bob Mills was coerced into working on the cart. When all the bodies had been loaded they hauled the heavy cart into the Main Camp and over to the crematorium, where he actually witnessed emaciated corpses being fed into the ovens—a sight he will never forget. Otherwise, as he recalls, life went on in the Little Camp.

> We now had one appell per day. This was in the evening and as before lasted from two to three hours. We all received one blanket each and a clean shirt—another was issued about four weeks later. We also had a shower which everyone enjoyed immensely. Our hair was kept clipped short, much to our annoyance, but we found it easier to keep clean. We had to go to the kitchens and carry back all the food for the block as the Frenchmen who were our block-mates had to work from dawn until 6 p.m. In wet weather this was quite a job as the ground became very slippery and muddy, but we had to either do it or starve. When the weather became colder we were given a topcoat each and this helped enormously for going out into the cold, as we had to get up at 4.30 a.m. if we wished to have our morning coffee and collect our daily bread ration.

Life for the airmen had now settled into a monotonous pattern of rollcalls every night, the same meagre and insubstantial food ration, and each of the men becoming worried at their continual weight loss. Fleas and bedbugs proved a constant source of irritation and the men itched incessantly, willing themselves not to scratch, for the smallest open sore invited infection. With no medicine or nutritious food these wounds would not heal and became weeping, open sores. The men soon learned to stuff any such holes in their flesh with small wedges of paper to soak up the matter. Tom Blackham had a suppurating cut five centimetres round and deep.

Welshman Terry Gould from Caerphilly was shot down over France on 2 June 1944, just four days before D-Day. He has some very vivid memories of his time in Buchenwald.

> It was like hell to us, we saw so many atrocities. People were dying all the time through lack of nourishment and typhus. The cremations of the dead took place every Wednesday and Friday. We always knew the day because that day we had half-rations of soup as they took our fuel for the crematorium. One day a police officer who had collaborated with the Germans in Poland was brought into the camp. There were about 30 or 40 Poles there and they recognised and lynched him. He was soon dead.

The men would spend all day sitting outside on the ground, filling in the long daylight hours with desultory conversation and an occasional doze in the sunshine. They knew the days were growing shorter and cooler and they would soon be spending most of the time on the wooden bunks in their barracks, which seemed to grow even harder as the flesh wilted from their bodies.

By now the airmen had acquired and carefully guarded their own food bowls, known in the camp as gammels. These were an absolute necessity if one was to receive a portion of the day's watery soup. No gammel, no food—it was a hard fact of life in the camp, and thieves were constantly on the lookout for spare bowls in order to obtain extra rations.

Every Thursday the men had to wash out their barracks and the shelves on which they slept under the supervision of their block altester, and cover the floor with quicklime. This gave off a pungent chlorine smell, but at least it provided some small means of maintaining hygiene. However, if there was no sunshine that day the bunks did not dry out and the damp would seep through thin blankets, striking at shoulders and hips.

Eric Johnston was suffering terrible pain, caused by a huge pus-filled whitlow on his right heel. It was so inflamed and causing him so much agony that a medical orderly was called to the block. The men, especially Eric, did not expect much in the way of medical treatment— nor did he receive it. The begrudging orderly who finally arrived treated the wound quickly and painfully by cutting into Eric's heel and digging out the whitlow without any thought of antiseptic. Eric winced and groaned, but at least he had received some form of treatment. The orderly casually bound the foot with toilet paper and left. There were certainly no bandages to be had, but toilet paper dressing was changed periodically. At least it was clean and relatively sterile.

One day a party of 500 Jews who had been brought into Buchenwald were massed for despatch to Auschwitz. These men had been forced to work in a synthetic petrol factory near Leipzig, and some had been burned terribly when the factory was bombed by the Americans. These terrified individuals were marched to the railway station and crushed into four cattle trucks. Those close to death and unable to walk to the siding were piled onto carts drawn by other prisoners, who were forced to push them along Caracho Road at double time. The strongest in the carts struggled feebly to raise their heads from beneath the pile of dying and dead, but many died on the trip to the station. Their bodies were simply flung through the open doors of the cattle trucks. One Pole who attempted to escape was easily captured and hung in front of the others—as an example. The hanging was a clumsy affair, and the Pole took a full five minutes to die.

In September 1700 Danes, mostly police officials, arrived at Buchenwald and were placed into huts near the airmen. They had not only refused to cooperate with the German occupation forces in Denmark, but had supported the Resistance's acts of sabotage and had proved to be something of an embarrassment while imprisoned in their homeland. According to Ray Perry they were 'a fine looking body of men, but the rigours of life in a concentration camp would soon take their toll.'

While generally keeping to themselves and avoiding illegal undertakings against their captors, the Danes proved to be of immeasurable assistance to their fellow prisoners by providing some food items from the Red Cross parcels they were permitted to receive. Later a group of 350 Norwegian students found themselves cast into Buchenwald, and they too were appalled at the conditions and circumstances of the camp.

While acts of grossest perversity were committed daily throughout the camp, and shock soon gave way to a numbing inurement, there would be no more soul-destroying experience for the airmen to witness than the day the SS, without prior warning, hauled the remaining 250 gypsy children from Block 58, herded them into a group, and surrounded them with carbine-bearing guards.

These poor innocent children, many of whom had suffered castration at the hands of unfeeling butchers in the medical block, cried and called out for their frantic fathers or relatives, who were held at bay by blows from carbines or machine pistols. The heart-rending sobbing and screaming still haunts many an inmate who was witness to the events of that dark day. Those children without family cried out for friends who had protected and tended them in camp, either for reasons of compassion or even sexual gratification, while the adults moaned and wept for the children they knew they would never see again.

The crying and screaming children were hustled into a long pantechnicon vehicle, and the back of the van was then closed. For the rest of that day an ominous silence hung over the camp, save for the distraught weeping of loved ones. It was a day of barbarism and tragedy no one who was there wishes to remember... or can ever forget. It was later rumoured, but never confirmed, that the pantechnicon was in fact an elaborate gas chamber similar to others in use in Germany at that time, and that the gypsy children were dead before the vehicle even left Buchenwald.

*   *   *

William Powell from Arizona, one of the USAAF airmen, was devastated to find a young Belgian in the camp hospital who had assisted him after being shot down.

> The young man had been a contact for me in Brussels after a crew member and I had walked to there in an attempt to get back. I saw him at Buchenwald in a so-called hospital, shot with typhus and on the verge of death. Both legs had to be amputated and of course he died, leaving a wife and three children. I did not realise what war could do to a country until I was forced to parachute out of our plane and then evade capture for seven months with the aid of the Belgian people. Their lives were on the line every day, as well as not having any freedom.
>
> In a small town near Brugelette there was a farm run by a girl of about eighteen and her mother. I did not stay with them but was living on a farm next door. This woman and her mother, in spite of a German garrison which was quartered in a large house less than a mile from the farm, had up to seven Allied flyers hidden on the farm. They even held a church service for the crew of a downed B-17 that fell near the farm. After I left, the mother and daughter were picked up by the Gestapo and imprisoned, then sent on a train to a concentration camp. Fortunately the Americans broke through and liberated the train. The girl's father was already a prisoner of the Germans.
>
> I came to admire the Belgian people very much as they really resisted their country's occupation to the fullest extent. It must take a lot of dedication and courage to put your life on the line.

6

In the Valley of the Shadow

For a nation so meticulously precise in its wartime documentation of its prisoners, the Germans somehow allowed a captured enemy agent of extraordinary talent to pull the wool over their collective eyes and eventually escape from their clutches.

The remarkable story of Wing Commander Forest Frederick Edward (Tommy) Yeo-Thomas, RAFVR, GC, MC and Bar, Legion d'Honeur and Croix de Guerre has been told before, particularly in Bruce Marshall's *The White Rabbit*. Little is mentioned, however, of the prominent part he played in the lives and ultimate salvation of the airmen at Buchenwald, so it is worth recounting in brieg this man's remarkable story prior to his arrival as a prisoner at the concentration camp.

Tommy Yeo-Thomas was born in London's Holborn area on 17 June 1901, but was educated for the most part in France. A determined and highly temperamental youth, his unorthodox behaviour saw him expelled from schools in both France and England. At age sixteen he managed to bluff his way into military service by claiming to be two years older, and served with the Allied armies until the end of the 1914–18 war.

His first experiences of war came to what he later described as 'a premature end' with the signing of the Armistice, and in seeking out further action he sided with the Poles in their fight against the Russians over the following two years. He was taken by the Bolsheviks, but in the first of his many daring escapes, and displaying the boldness exemplified in his later adventures, he managed to flee from a daybreak appointment with a firing squad.

In 1920 he returned to Paris and worked at a variety of positions before joining the renowned dressmaking firm of Molyneux in 1932, where he eventually became one of the directors. However, the song of war still enticed Yeo-Thomas over the years, and once he even contemplated enlistment in the French Foreign Legion. Instead he offered his services to the Royal Air Force, who took him on as an interpreter. Following a period of relative inactivity he became an Intelligence Officer, entering the RF (French Resistance) section of Special Operations Executive under Captain Piquet-Wicks. This section organised the supply and parachuting of arms and equipment to the various Resistance movements across France, and the transport of covert agents to and from that country.

On 23 February 1943 Yeo-Thomas was parachuted into France on his first operation for SOE under the code name 'White Rabbit', later returning to England with an American Air Force officer he had rescued. On his second mission into France on 17 September that year he obtained valuable information for his bosses back in London, evading capture on no fewer than six occasions. He returned to England eight weeks later.

By now Yeo-Thomas was starting to court the odds, but his audacity drove him on. On his next assignment into enemy territory he was betrayed to the Gestapo, who gave him a savage beating. He then underwent four days of continuous interrogation, interspersed with floggings and torture. The vicious treatment included immersing him head-downwards in ice-cold water with his arms and legs chained. These interrogations went on for two months, but he stuck to his cover story that he was simply a downed airman by the name of Kenneth Dodkin. The real Squadron Leader Dodkin had worked with Yeo-Thomas back in England, coaching him at length on his life and service history. The Germans were not entirely convinced with Yeo-Thomas' story and offered him his freedom in exchange for information on the head of a Resistance group, but the prisoner kept reiterating that he was Dodkin. Eventually he contracted blood poisoning from the chains which cut into his wrists and came close to losing his left arm.

After two daring but unsuccessful attempts to escape, Yeo-Thomas was transported to Fresnes prison, where he spent four months in Cell 293 in the 2nd Division, receiving further interrogation and very little food. Throughout these months of almost incessant maltreatment he refused to give information beyond Dodkin's name, rank and service number. Any snippets that he deliberately let slip related to Dodkin's past. He knew full well that the German intelligence people would have checked these details and found them correct.

Whatever their doubts, the Germans felt sure their prisoner was an enemy agent, but they seemed to decide that he was small fry in the order of things and eventually transferred 'Dodkin' to Compeigne prison with a group of captured operatives. He made two escape attempts before he and 36 other prisoners were called out and sent under heavy guard to Buchenwald. On the way they stopped for three days at Saarbrucken, where they were beaten and confined to a tiny hut. They reached Buchenwald on 17 August 1944—just three days before the arrival of the group of airmen.

After registration the 37 agents were placed into Block 17, an isolated hut surrounded by barbed wire, containing 380 prisoners. As soon as they were settled in their quarters Yeo-Thomas held a council to coordinate their future escape activities. In the afternoon he met with two fellow SOE operatives already in the camp, Maurice Pertchuk and Christopher Burney, both of whom he knew well. He also made contact with two Russian colonels through one of his British officers who spoke Bulgarian, and talked with them at length about the need to smuggle in arms to back up an escape attempt. Yeo-Thomas knew his group was there under sentence of execution, and speed in arranging such matters was imperative. On 20 August came the welcome news that a large contingent of British and American airmen had arrived at the camp and were undergoing arrival formalities at the administrative area. Yeo-Thomas set about talking with the senior officer of these men as soon as possible.

When Yeo-Thomas eventually met with Phil Lamason, he introduced himself by his assumed identity of Squadron Leader Ken Dodkin. From then on, to his complete bewilderment, things did not seem to go at all well; the New Zealander instantly became suspicious and non-committal. As it turned out, Lamason knew the real Dodkin quite well, having carried him on two missions before the fellow became non-operational, but Lamason was not about to let on. Lamason was then introduced to Christopher Burney, in whom he felt he could confide. When they were alone he informed the SOE agent that the prisoner pretending to be Dodkin was in fact an imposter. Burney was surprised that Lamason knew the real Dodkin, and quickly assured him that things were in order, saying there was a very valid reason for the use of the alias. Thereafter, Lamason always referred to Yeo-Thomas as Dodkin, but was one of the very few men who knew the brash Englishman's true identity.

According to his biographer Bruce Marshall, Yeo-Thomas was able to establish a firm friendship and close working relationship with Lamason. It was essential for the common good of the men under their command.

To Yeo-Thomas the arrival of these new recruits for his army seemed providential. Not only with a potential of more than 200 men at his disposal was he now in a better position to bargain with the Russians, but the fact that the majority were trained flyers appeared little short of miraculous.

About twelve kilometres from Buchenwald, he had learned, was a small and poorly guarded airfield called Hohra. Provided they could fight their way out of Buchenwald, he was soon persuading Lamason, there would be little to prevent their attacking the airfield, seizing the bombers and flying back to the Allied lines. The combined forces of themselves and the Russians would be divided up into units of ten, this time not according to nationality, but with a pilot, navigator, air-gunner, engineer and radio operator in each team. Lamason, as hot-headed as Tommy, readily agreed.

There seemed to be only two stumbling-blocks; one was the presence in Lamason's group of a so-called American flyer suspected to have been planted there as a stool pigeon, and who would require to be kept in ignorance of their plan and watched [see below]; and the other was the lack of arms. But even the latter was not insuperable: there were, Yeo-Thomas had discovered, arms in the camp, but only the Communist leaders knew where they were concealed, and so far all his attempts to make them divulge this secret had failed.

Lamason states that the unsubstantiated reference to the American flyer should have been deleted from Marshall's book to forestall any undeserved postwar suspicion falling on the KLB American airmen contingent. The flyer in question was not an American, but their Dutch translator, who had been observed talking privately to some of the German guards. This man, as with all the KLB airmen of all nationalities, proved to be completely trustworthy and beyond suspicion.

Above: Goethe's tree in the camp's compound. The prisoners believed that when the tree fell, so too would Hitler's Third Reich.

(Photo: Musée de la Resistance et de la Deportation, Besancon).

Below: Karl and Ilse Koch on their wedding day.
(Photo: Yad Vashem, Israel)

Buchenwald's Kleinelager (Little Camp), a quarantine area housing the contingent of airmen. *(Photo: Buchenwald Memorial Museum).*

Wing Commander F.F.E. Yeo-Thomas the famed 'White Rabbit'. *(Photo: Barbara Yeo-Thomas)*

A reconnaissance photo taken of Buchenwald concentration camp just prior to the bombing raid of August 1944. The quarantine area known as the Little Camp is out of photo, to the rear of the prisoners' barracks.

1. Gustloff Armament Works (GAW) **2.** SS Officers' and Troop Area **3.** German Barracks **4.** Riding Academy **5.** German Armament Works (DAW) **6.** Gatehouse and Main Tower **7.** Appell Platz (Rollcall Compound) **8.** Crematorium **9.** Headquarters Area **10.** Prisoners' Barracks **11.** Camp zoo **12.** Goethe's Oak **13.** SS Garages **14.** Kommandant's Villa

(Photo: National Air and Space Museum, Washington, DC)

With incredible accuracy, American bombers destroyed two armaments
plants huddled against the concentration camp, and many of the camp's
administration buildings.
(Photo: National Air and Space Museum, Washington, DC)

Below: After the air raid came the massive task of clearing up the
devastation. *(Photo: Musée de la Resistance et de la Deportation,
Besancon)*

Then tragedy struck. On 9 September 1944 an announcement blared out over the camp's tannoy system, ordering sixteen of Yeo-Thomas' men to report to the bunker in the watchtower. The men named were assembled and taken away, fully expecting to return after some type of formality. One of the men, a Canadian named Frank Pickersgill, led the men in singing 'It's a Long Way to Tipperary' as they were led away. On arrival at the tower they were told they were to be executed, and then thrown into the bunker for the night. A priest, attempting to give the Roman Catholics among them extreme unction, was denied access to the condemned men. He could hear sounds of the men being savagely beaten, but there was nothing he could do. The following day they were removed from the bunker for a few minutes, only to be thrown back in again.

The sixteen were then taken across to the wooden mortuary block. Once inside they were tied in pairs by the hands, standing back to back. Nooses made from piano wire were placed around their necks, and each pair of men were hoisted aloft until the nooses engaged over steel hooks protruding from the walls. They died a violent, agonising death, thrashing about as the nooses bit deeply into their necks. Once their struggles had ceased they were lifted down, their death verified, and the bodies sent upstairs for incineration in the crematorium's ovens.

Once news of the murder of his men had been confirmed, Yeo-Thomas initiated a desperate scheme to save as many of the remaining agents as possible. He had earlier been approached by the political prisoner Eugen Kogon, who had been in Buchenwald since September 1939, and Professor Alfred Balachowsky of the Pasteur Institute in Paris, whose work at the camp included an attempt to produce an anti-typhus vaccine. Both men worked together in Block 50 on medical experiments. They had persuaded Sturmbannfuehrer Ding-Schuler, the head of Block 46, that an Allied victory was imminent and that he should try to save the lives of some of the British agents. Ding-Schuler had been injecting deadly viruses into the prisoners with impunity and he knew he would be called to account for his heinous crimes after the war. He finally gave in. The plan called for the agents to assume the identities of French prisoners already dying of typhus in the hospital ward, but Ding-Schuler felt he could not hide more than a few substitutions without arousing suspicion, and stated that he could help no more than three men. Balachowsky brought the news to Yeo-Thomas, and told him that

Ding-Schuler had placed a further condition on the scheme. He had demanded that as 'Dodkin' was leader of the agents, and therefore the most potent voice in later pleas for clemency, he was to be one of the three men saved. He was quite unmoving in this condition, and so it was left to Yeo-Thomas to select the other two men—a fearful decision to place on any man. Who should be saved, and who must die?

Yeo-Thomas went into seclusion to ponder his decision, and to select the two men who might have the best chance for survival. Finally he sought out Balachowsky and gave him the names of two men who spoke fluent French, thereby giving the scheme the best possible chance of success. Balachowsky nodded and went off to see Ding-Schuler with the news. The men Yeo-Thomas had chosen were Henri (Harry) Peleuve and Stephane Hessel.

The French prisoners terminally ill with typhus had recently arrived at the camp as part of a large group and were in a special ward of the Revier. A German Kapo by the name of Arthur Dietzsch had also been promised confirmation of his action to save the men should he be brought to trial, and he arranged for some to be transferred to Block 46. Among them were three desperately ill men by the names of Marcel Seigneur, Maurice Chouquet and Michel Boitel. These brave men, who knew they were dying, agreed to the substitution. Meanwhile Yeo-Thomas, Peleuve and Hessel were given injections which would produce a high fever and were transferred to Block 46 after Dietzsch had 'diagnosed' typhus.

The deception was carried out just in time. On 4 October the tannoy blared once again and the names of a further fifteen from Tommy Yeo-Thomas' group were read out, including that of Captain Peleuve. He was immediately injected with more drugs to simulate typhus. When Kommandant Pister was told that one of the condemned fifteen was desperately ill with typhus he ordered Ding-Schuler to release the man so that he could be eliminated along with the others. Fortunately for Peleuve, Ding-Schuler was able to convince Pister that to do so might cause an epidemic throughout camp. Pister reluctantly compromised, saying that Peleuve had to be killed immediately by injection.

An NCO was despatched to carry out Peleuve's execution, but Dietzsch managed to waylay the man with a bottle of schnapps, and when the soldier was drunk showed him a typhus-racked patient and identified him as Peleuve. Dietzsch dismissed the use of a lethal injection, saying it was a waste of medicine—the man would obviously be dead by morning. Agreeing with Dietzsch, the drunken NCO left and reported that the execution had been carried out.

The other fourteen agents whose names had been read out were taken to the mortuary block, knowing their last moments were upon them. They were murdered in the same callous fashion as their colleagues.

By the following morning Marcel Seigneur was found to have died, and Peleuve assumed his identity, while Seigneur's body was cremated as that of the SOE agent. It had been a close thing. Maurice Boitel died on 13 October, and Chouquet five days later: Yeo-Thomas and Hessel took their respective identities. Again this was none too soon, for their execution orders had come through.

Now in the guise of Frenchmen, the three men still had to survive until the Allied liberation, but Kogon was able to help once again by having the men transferred to work parties on outside Kommandos. All three men would survive the war.

Sadly, the memories of Fresnes and Buchenwald would haunt Peleuve through the postwar years. He married and had two children, but was later divorced. He took on a position as the overseas manager for a light engineering company, but a deep melancholy had set in and he died a broken man in Seville on 18 March 1963.

The other four surviving agents, twin brothers Henry and Alfred Newton, Maurice Southgate and Christopher Burney, lived in constant fear of following the other 30 men to their deaths, but somehow their execution orders never came through.

Kapo Dietzsch missed the gallows because of the written testament promised him by Wing Commander Yeo-Thomas, but was sentenced to life imprisonment. Major Ding-Schuler took his own life in September 1945, before going on trial.

For his courage and insuperable example, Tommy Yeo-Thomas was awarded the George Cross on 15 February 1946, and the words of his citation perhaps best relate his movements after Buchenwald.

Wing Commander Yeo-Thomas was later transferred to a work Kommando for Jews. In attempting to escape he was picked up by a German patrol and, claiming French nationality, was transferred to another camp near Marienburg for French prisoners of war. On 16 April 1945 he led a party of 20 in a most gallant attempt to escape in broad daylight. Ten were killed by fire from the guards. Those who reached cover split up into smaller groups. Wing Commander Yeo-Thomas became separated from his companions after three days without food. He continued alone for a week and was recaptured when only 800 yards from the American lines. A few days later he escaped with a party of ten French prisoners of war, whom he led through German patrols to the American lines.

Wing Commander Yeo-Thomas thus turned his final mission into a success by his determined opposition to the enemy, his strenuous efforts to maintain the morale of his fellow prisoners, and his brilliant escape activities. He endured brutal treatment and torture without flinching and showed the most amazing fortitude and devotion to duty throughout his service abroad, during which he was under the constant threat of death.

Yeo-Thomas returned to Paris after the war, becoming a representative of the Federation of British Industries, but the treatment he had received at the hands of the Germans meant he was never physically the same person. Gradually his health deteriorated and he died on 26 February 1964.

It would be certain that his widow Barbara mused a little as the grand tributes flowed during his Memorial Service at St Clement's Dane Church on 30 April that year. When her husband died at the age of 62 he had never been compensated for the evil perpetrated upon him. The British government had granted their famed White Rabbit a disability pension, but this barely covered his medical expenses. At the time of his death his own government had done virtually nothing towards obtaining just compensation from the Germans.

During the compilation of this book Barbara Yeo-Thomas spoke to the author at length about her husband, and mentioned the manner in which he was portrayed in *The White Rabbit*.

If I may make just one comment on Bruce Marshall's characterisation of Tommy: to me Tommy was sunshine and laughter; he had a wonderful sense of humour and quick repartee. I don't think this comes across somehow. Admittedly there was the icy steel side to his nature, but one man who was with him in Buchenwald told me, 'We would be feeling as miserable as Hell, then Tommy would come along, looking awful, but with a broad grin on his face, and somehow we all felt better, although there was absolutely nothing to laugh about!' I understand what this man meant—Tommy had a sort of charisma; it was impossible to be depressed or unhappy when he was around.

Three of the surviving SOE operatives—Burney, Peleuve and Southgate—have since died, but Stephane Hessel carried on to become a French Ambassador and he too requested a few lines to be able to pay tribute to his former colleague.

Of all the qualities that made up the exceptional figure of Wing Commander Yeo-Thomas, the one that remains most unforgettably in my memory is his sense of humour; in the truly dramatic situations we faced together, at times when life and death, torture or salvation were in the most precarious balance, he would smilingly bet for success and take us with him with a joke. From him I have learnt not only courage and determination, but the courteous bow to the Goddess of Fortune without whose help our thriving meets frustration. He had needed her often and she never failed him, and we who fought by his side felt through him her protection and goodwill.

As a Frenchman I should have been doubly grateful for the way he, as a Briton, chose to save my life. But it seemed natural since his belonging to France as much as to his own country was part of his nature and, may I say, part of his charm.

*   *   *

On 27 September 1944 Flying Officer Philip Hemmens succumbed to septicaemia, rheumatic fever and pneumonia, and died in his sleep. When he first developed septicaemia he was placed in the hospital, but nothing was done except that his joints were opened up using a knife. He didn't have the strength left to fight off the subsequent infection, and the constant damp and cold only served to compound his illness. His body was cremated and the ashes stored in a vault already crammed to overflowing with small labelled bottles.

Philip, the son of the Rev. Ernest Hemmens, had served with No. 49 (Lancaster) Squadron RAF before being shot down over France. Ron Leverington, in hiding at the time with fellow crew members Douglas Eagle, Reg Joyce and Don Leslie at the home of their helper Madame Hugette Verhague, recalls that Hemmens, who suffered a broken arm in the crash of the Lancaster, often paid them a visit.

Philip's arm seemed to be progressing satisfactorily while we were in hiding, and on occasions he accompanied myself and Hugette on night sorties in the forest nearby, looking for likely landing and dropping points in the clearings. He did manage to get hold of a plan of a V-1 site, which was very sketchy, on a piece of paper which he hid in his sack. We ate this in Gestapo headquarters before being searched. He was a great guy.

When he entered Buchenwald the month before his death Hemmens was, apart from his broken arm, a picture of physical fitness. He lost his life not only through illness, but through the criminal neglect and incompetence of those who manned the so-called hospital. When his fellow airmen had learned of his death a memorial service was organised and held outside Hut 58, conducted by one of the Danish fathers before a solemn group of prisoners with cropped heads bared, standing respectfully at attention. All 1700 of the Danish prisoners attended the service and Flying Officer Tommy Blackham gave a memorial address in English. A minute's silence was then observed, following which the hymns 'Abide with Me' and 'Nearer my God to Thee' were sung in an emotional mixture of French, Danish, Norwegian and English, which lent a sweeping poignancy to the service for the gallant young flier.

*   *   *

A week after Hemmens' death, conditions began to improve a little for the men. Their shoes were returned, and they were issued with some short coats. This was certainly the work of several of the more seasoned inmates, and not the SS. The clothing was not officially issued, but as the longer serving Communist prisoners practically ran day-to-day administration within the camp, small concessions could be made in exchange for favours or gifts.

Time lay heavily in the men's hearts as the weather grew colder. October brought with it chilling winds and constant, driving rain. The men spent most of their time inside the barracks, and by night, although packed tightly together, they still suffered from the biting cold. Stanley Booker echoed a common fear from those days of uncertainty.

Our main worry was that nobody knew we were there. None of us had been caught by the Luftwaffe in the first place, and there had been no contact with the International Red Cross at Paris, or anywhere else. We all knew the war was going well, but we could not contemplate that anyone could possibly know where we were, and thus we might simply disappear without trace.

To address the constant stress, apprehension and feelings of insecurity expressed by the KLB airmen it was decided they should hold formal meetings to give them a sense of purpose and order in their lives. And so in October 1944 the KLB [Konzentrationlager Buchenwald] Club came into being. Elected representatives of each nationality held separate meetings to collate the previously scattered efforts of those who had proposed address lists, meetings after the war and other pursuits. The meetings were held in accordance with strict protocol and were well attended. More than anything else, they displayed the airmen's militariness and solidarity, and though few of their recommendations were adopted after the war, they formed a bond that brings the men together even today, half a century after the liberation of Buchenwald.

The man elected as the East Canada representative, Flying Officer Art Kinnis, carefully compiled a list containing the names, ranks, service numbers, Buchenwald numbers and private addresses of all 168 airmen.

Thirty-five years later, in 1979, Art Kinnis saw a photograph of four former Buchenwald Canadians and hauled out his almost-forgotten address list. The four men's wartime addresses were there, and one by one he managed to make contact with Jim Stewart, Stan Hetherington, Ed Carter-Edwards and Bill Gibson. Art and his wife Betty packed themselves into their mobile motorhome and crossed Canada, meeting the men and picking up new contact addresses along the way. By the time he returned to Victoria, British Columbia, he had decided to embark on the vast and complex task of tracing as many of the airmen as possible—men who had relocated themselves all over the world. His list is far from complete, and sadly bears the stark notation of 'deceased' against many names, but at the time of writing a spirit of comradeship has been rekindled, and men who have not met or corresponded for nearly 50 years are now back in contact.

For the sake of posterity, it is worth recording here the minutes of the meetings attended and notated by Art Kinnis, for they trace the origins of the group known as the KLB Club.

Meeting held in Block 58, Buchenwald
Date: 12th October 1944, 1630 hours
Chairman: F/O A. Kinnis

Following in the footsteps of the USA and British members, the Canadians present at Buchenwald decided to get together and do whatever was possible towards the formation of a Canadian club which would keep alive the comradeship shown in the last three months. F/O J. Prudham was nominated for President by F/O C. Willis and seconded by F/O C. Hoffman. Motion carried unanimously.

At this point it was suggested by the Chairman that as members could be divided into three main groups, namely 15 in the east, 6 from the central and 6 from the west, that one member from each regional group be on the Central Committee. This being agreed upon, the following members were duly elected by their respective groups:

EAST Montreal: F/O J. D. Harvie
Toronto: F/O E. C. Watson
CENTRAL Winnipeg: F/O T. R. Hodgson
WEST Vancouver: F/O A. G. Kinnis

Suggestions were requested by the committee and members were told that further meetings would be held in which any ideas would be greatly appreciated. It had been suggested that in view of the great distance that Canadians would have to travel for a central meeting that all would find it more practical to have regional meetings, with the local leader in charge. If at all possible a central gathering will be attempted every five years. Full cooperation with American members as well as affiliation with the Canadian Legion will be one of several aims.

Meeting adjourned.

The Committee of the British Members is:
President: F/Lt T. Blackham
Secretary: F/O R. Taylor
Members: F/O M. Mutter
F/O E. Jackson
F/O K. Chapman

The problems of the Australian members are such that one member only was elected, said man being F/Sgt E. L. Johnston. They will keep in touch with all chapters through him.

The Committee of the United States members is:

President: 1st Lt W. Powell
Secretary: 2nd Lt R. H. Brown

Meeting held in Block 58, Buchenwald
Date: 13th October 1944, 1000 hours
Chairman: F/O J. Prudham

At this meeting the Committee approved of the following constitution which will be subject to the Club's approval:

1. That the name of the Club shall be the KLB Club, and that membership shall include those Allied flying personnel who were prisoners at Buchenwald.
2. That the Committee shall consist of:
   a) a President, whose duties shall be to call and preside over all meetings.
   b) a Vice President who will act in the absence of the President.
   c) a Secretary/Treasurer who will be the Managing Director.
   d) Regional Members—elected in the following manner: 2 from the east, 1 from the central, and 1 from the west.
   e) an NCO member.
3. As seen by Section 2d, Canada has been divided into three regional groups—east, central and west. This is due to the small membership, and their distribution, and the great distance all would have to travel. It is proposed that each regional chairman be responsible for his own region's gatherings.
4. A pin and a membership list shall be sent to all members, said list to have the name, address and occupation of all Allied personnel. The list will be revised where necessary.
5. An initiation fee of $15.00 shall be charged, with an annual fee of $1.
6. A souvenir booklet shall be issued to all members.
7. Full cooperation with the American Club will be attempted, and the Canadian Branch will strive to affiliate itself with the Canadian Legion.
8. A bank account shall be opened in the name of the KLB Club, and the Secretary or President shall be authorised to sign checks up to the sum of $15.00, and by the Secretary and President if over that amount.

It is proposed that a national meeting be held every five years for the purpose of selection of officers. If possible this should be held in conjunction with the American Club. The purpose of the Club is to perpetuate the comradeship already shown by the flying personnel of Great Britain, Australia, United States and Canada by the interchanging of pamphlets, ideas and visits.

Meeting held in Block 58, Buchenwald
Date: 13th October 1944, 1400 hours
Chairman: F/O J. Prudham

The second meeting of the Club was for the ratification of the proposed constitution. Full approval was obtained.

Members were asked to contribute sketches or ideas for the international pin.

It was further suggested that a gathering be held in London as soon after our return as possible. All members should leave their full address (home and abroad) at BC House, Waterloo Place, London. The Secretary will pick up all information at that point.

The meeting adjourned.

1st International Committee Meeting
15th October 1944
Chairman: F/Lt T. Blackham

It has been suggested that a book in the nature of a history of our life from Fresnes prison to our stay in Buchenwald be compiled as a souvenir.

The Committee drew up the following rough plan:-

1) Cover of blue leather with the club pin embossed in silver or gold.
2) A flyleaf dedicated to F/O Philip Hemmens.
3) A list of club officers.
4) Editorial.
5) Photograph of all aircraft flown by the various club members.
6) History of all our activity from Fresnes.
7) History of the various sections (humorous).
8) Photographs of all members in uniform (no hat).
9) Photograph with prison number underneath; name and nickname; rank; service number; position in type of aircraft flown; date shot down and captured. Date of birth, married or single, address and occupation.
10) Motto: 'Appell is Appell'.

International Committee Meeting
17 October 1944

Full approval was obtained in the selection of a pin design. All members expressed themselves as well pleased with the design.

The pin design formulated in Buchenwald is now a symbol that binds the airmen. It shows a naked, winged foot, symbolising their barefoot condition while in the concentration camp. The foot is chained to a ball bearing the letters KLB, with the whole mounted on a white star, which was the crest of the Allied invasion forces.

K·L·B CLUB

The Russians, through Phil Lamason's friendly overtures to their leaders, were supplying the airmen with some bread and clogs. Doctor Balachowski was meanwhile able to supplement the men's meagre diet; among experiments in which he was involved at the medical block were studies on rabbits, which were injected with various disease germs. When the rabbits died, and if the experiments had not rendered the animals uneatable, he secretly passed the carcasses on to the airmen who furtively cooked them.

It was about this time that specific orders from Berlin reached the desk of Kommandant Pister, who reluctantly set the process in motion. The orders stated that all of the airmen, including the bed-ridden and desperately ill, were to be exterminated within the week.

This terrible news was conveyed to Phil Lamason by a German Communist who had been given the information by a friend who worked in the administrative area. Lamason sought out Yeo-Thomas, Burney and Jan Robert, a Dutch patriot who had been an Olympic training masseur. The four men discussed the information at length, but concluded that there was precious little any of them could do to avert the mass execution. Talks with the Russians regarding weapons and armed resistance were coming along, albeit slowly. It was an inch-by-inch process, and a sudden demand for help would probably see the shutters go down on any further negotiations.

Christopher Burney told Lamason that, through contacts within the camp, he would try to pass a message concerning the airmen's plight to the outside world, but their only real hope at that time was to pray that the news was wrong. Lamason kept the information to himself, and in fact did not reveal the closeness of the airmen's escape from extermination until a KLB reunion in Canada in 1985.

There is little reason to doubt that the orders were issued, but the administration involved in carrying out such a vast and complex operation was massive. The airmen were certainly an embarrassment to the Germans, but their deaths would have enormous ramifications if the British found out. The killings would have to be concealed by the issue of false certificates stating that each death was the result of natural causes. Fortunately for the sake of the airmen, such documentation would require a great deal of time. Unaware of their pending extermination the airmen went about their daily routine.

*   *   *

How then did the miracle occur? How did the airmen secure a transfer from Buchenwald, when the records clearly state they were never to be transferred to another camp? The man to thank is Christopher Burney, the SOE agent and official camp interpreter. Burney, a former commando subaltern, was captured at Caen in August 1942 after being parachuted into France by SOE's 'F' Section. His German captors knew his identity, but despite interrogations and torture he refused to divulge anything other than his name, rank and number. He was cast into a solitary confinement cell for eighteen months, but he managed to survive this terrible ordeal and was sent to Buchenwald. For fifteen months, until the liberation of the camp, he was fully engaged in plans to seize control from the Germans.

His plans were continually frustrated by the German Communist prisoners who were forming their own resistance movement, and who thwarted his every attempt to obtain arms. These the International Camp Committee kept to themselves, and even regarded the young Englishman's plans with considerable mistrust and contempt.

As interpreter, Burney had free access to the Little Camp, and he was both a solace and an inspiration to the Allied airmen. He was in frequent contact with Wing Commander Yeo-Thomas, and was instrumental in organising the substitution affair for Tommy and his two companions, following which they hid out in Hut 46 until their transfer out of Buchenwald on a working party.

Being officially confined to the Little Camp, the airmen were not permitted into the Main Camp except for ration collection and various other fatigues or for administrative reasons. However, as the men's senior officer, Lamason was able to move into the Main Camp where he would meet and liaise discreetly with Burney and members of the powerful International Camp Committee. They decided to smuggle out a note, to be delivered to the Luftwaffe hierarchy, to let them know that aircrew personnel were being illegally held in a concentration camp.

With the aid of a trusted prisoner on an outside working party at the nearby Luftwaffe airfield the Committee managed to get their message out of the camp, with a request that an officer pass the information to Berlin, and for the Luftwaffe to intercede on behalf of the men.

The message apparently got through, for shortly after an outraged Hermann Goering made stern approaches 'at the highest level' and having exerted this pressure obtained the immediate transfer of the airmen to Luftwaffe control.

It had been a flimsy and perhaps risky chance, but it had paid off. Phil Lamason still recalls the time Yeo-Thomas informed him that the information had not only made it through to the Luftwaffe, but had in turn reached London.

'How on earth could you know it has reached England?' he enquired with disbelief.

Yeo-Thomas smiled. 'We heard it on the BBC news last night, courtesy of our secret radio,' was the laconic reply. 'You must learn to trust me, Phil. We'll soon have you and the other chaps out of here. Must go—talk with you later.' With that he walked off, leaving Lamason open-mouthed with incredulity.

*   *   *

On the morning of 14 October 1944 a tall, sharp-looking civilian arrived from Dulag Luft in Oberursel, the Luftwaffe's interrogation centre and transit camp for captured Allied aircrew, situated on the outskirts of Wiesbaden.

In the Little Camp, the puzzled airmen were ordered to assemble and told they were to be addressed in the Main Camp. With the exception of those in hospital they were marched down through the camp and taken to the large canteen building. The men were understandably nervous following the murders of the SOE people. Following on the heels of Phil Lamason they were herded into the canteen where the civilian stood facing them, accompanied by two Luftwaffe officers. For most of the men it was their first sight of a Luftwaffe uniform, and their desultory conversation swelled with speculation. The man held up his hands and called for silence.

'Gentlemen,' he began. 'I would ask that you listen very carefully to what I have to say. I am here from Dulag Luft. Do you all know where that is, and what it means?' He looked around as a few of the men murmured and nodded. They'd all heard of the centre where captured airmen were sent for interrogation prior to their transfer to more permanent POW camps.

'Recently, it came to the attention of the Luftwaffe that all of you were being held in this place and were brought here, so the SS tells me, by mistake!' A derisive howl greeted this statement, but the men quickly fell silent as the civilian raised his hand once again.

'Now I have brought you here for two reasons. The first is to tell you that you will all be released from this place and transferred to a prisoner of war camp—this time under Luftwaffe control.' The statement created an instant hubbub and this time it was Lamason who stood and requested silence.

'Thank you, Squadron Leader,' continued the civilian. 'I am also directed to inform you that this transfer is conditional on you completing the required information on some Red Cross forms. This is necessary to prove your identity and status, and must be fully completed. I am instructed to inform you that should any of you choose not to complete this formality you will remain at Buchenwald as a political prisoner, and I need hardly remind you what that might mean!'

It was apparent that the speaker could barely contain his disgust with the camp and its administrators. Together with the uniformed officers he brought forward a small stack of forms embossed with the Red Cross symbol and some pencils, which were passed around. As the men read the questionnaires they groaned in exasperation—these were the spurious forms they had been briefed on by the Intelligence people back in England. These forms not only required personal information but asked for details on their squadrons, aircraft and operational movements. Several of the men addressed themselves to Lamason.

'Sir, we've already been told not to fill out these bloody forms. What should we do?' Phil Lamason had already pondered the question and made his decision.

'We all know the origin of these forms,' he said to the small crowd now pressed around him. 'I will certainly not instruct any of you to go against orders. I'll just say this, that it is up to each man as to how much information he puts down, and how much of it is correct. I must however remind you that we are in an extremely dicey situation here [only Lamason knew of the extermination order at this time], and as we have been prisoners for several months now any information required on these forms is not only known to the Germans, but is out of date. For my own part I intend giving them nothing but my name, rank and number.'

The mood was one of confusion and anger, and one man confronted the German. 'It is against our orders to fill out this form. You know that as well as we do!'

The civilian's eyes blazed. 'You are not, repeat not, in a position to argue, young man. Either you fill in that form or you stay here. I am trying to help, but that help depends entirely upon you!'

It was a sticky situation. The men had no uniforms, no tags—nothing in fact to prove who they were. Was this German bluffing? The thought of remaining at the camp appalled the airmen, but how far could they go against King's regulations? Name, rank and service number only, the authorities in England had said. But had they ever envisaged a predicament such as the one in which the men now found themselves? The memories of their stay in camp, plus the prospect of winter, finally proved too much for the majority and they complied with the German's request, most of them following the advice of Lamason, which by now had been passed around. They wrote in their names and numbers and filled out the other information, for the most part with bogus addresses, squadrons and types of aircraft flown.

Texas-born Stratton Appleman was quite against Phil Lamason's recommendations. Appleman, who had flown a glider into Normandy before the beach landing on 6 June, had been captured in full uniform and made a prisoner of war. Two weeks later he escaped from a prison train bound for Germany. He and fellow airman Ralph Dearnay were hidden by the Resistance in the wine-producing village of Roseay. The two men, dressed in civilian attire, were arrested while attempting to make their way to Eparnay and an Underground escape route. Thus

Appleman had once been an officially recognised prisoner of war of Germany, but he too had lost all military status when joining the group bound for Buchenwald. Now he was adamant that the men should follow his example and only give the required name, rank and number.

As the senior officer, Lamason was taking a position now recognised by military authorities as the proper role for the senior officer among a group of POWs. His first concern was the welfare of his men. As a very junior officer who had seen that to follow my original military orders had seen me well through innumerable interrogations, I chose to challenge his order. I announced that I would do everything possible to report anyone who cooperated with the Germans in what I considered a violation of our standing military orders.

Several of the men sided with me in refusing to complete the forms. The German major present explained that those who cooperated would depart Buchenwald the following day, and that he could not be responsible for those who didn't.

If Lamason remembers the incident I describe, I hope he will remember my youth. My position during the past eighteen years as spokesman for the US Veterans' Administration has required me to become involved in extensive study of POW behaviour, and I recognise mine as a rather typical case of trying to restore self-esteem lost as a result of being a prisoner by trying to over comply with my own interpretation of military orders, and by drawing attention to my exploits as an escapee. With all that experience behind me, I know now that the KLB Club was fortunate to have Lamason as its leader.

For 30 of the men, the thought of aiding the Germans in any way, shape or form was repugnant, however dated the information they were asked to disclose might be. They stood firm and either gave only names and numbers, or totally refused to fill out the forms, enraging the civilian and his cronies, who separated these dissenters from the rest of the men as they handed back their uncompleted forms. Phil Lamason's countryman Malcolm Cullen was one of this number.

After the interview we were isolated from the remainder of our companions, and that night we turned and tossed in unaccustomed beds wondering if what we had done would prove to be our undoing. Next morning, however, we were more cheerful and decided amongst ourselves that we would hold to our first decision. Late that afternoon

Above: Liberating US soldiers were appalled to find hundreds of skeletal bodies piled up in the camp awaiting disposal.

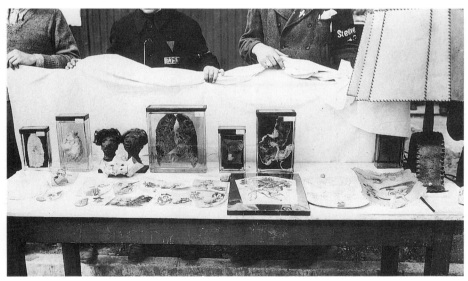

Bottom: Shrunken heads, lampshades and other grotesque items manufactured from the skin of inmates murdered for their tattoos made for a grim display following the liberation of Buchenwald in April 1945. *(Photos: Imperial War Museum, London)*

The camp's clock tower and entrance gates were preserved as part of the Buchenwald Memorial Museum. *(Photo: S. Booker).*

Below: Bob ('Lofty') Mills and his crew at the National Press Centre dinner in Canberra, 24 June 1988. (left to right) Bob Mills, Jim Gwilliam, Keith Mills, Ian Innes and Eric Johnston. *(Photo: C. Burgess)*

we were taken back and harangued again, this time individually. Finding that he still only received a polite negative from each of us, he finished up and informed us that it was the last we would see of him, and that he thought we would have had more sense.

I must say that as we marched away this time back to our old barrack, my spirits had reached a low ebb, and the thought of staying behind while most of the others were sent to a proper camp made me shudder!

The next few days passed slowly for the airmen, who waited impatiently for news of their fate. For those who had partially or totally refused to fill out the bogus form the days were filled with agonies of uncertainty.

Nothing was heard until 3 p.m. on the afternoon of 18 October when a list was sent to the block, naming those who were to report to the main gate the following morning. Only fourteen in hospital, who were too sick to move, were to remain behind. Malcolm Cullen and his fellow dissenters heard their names read out together with the others. The men could barely contain themselves at the thought that this might be their last night in the concentration camp.

No one slept very well that evening, and the following morning many were up early, endeavouring to shave themselves with the two or three well-used razors some men had managed to retain. The blades were blunt and it was raining outside, but they were too excited to care about such minor inconveniences. Not even the march to the Effektenkammer in the driving rain could dampen their spirits.

The men were handed their old civilian clothing, together with most effects taken from them on arrival at Buchenwald. Once again they shook their heads at German efficiency, although the clothes now hung like sacks from their emaciated forms. Outside, the SS guards stood them in files of five and conducted a headcount in the rain, which had now slackened off to a drizzle.

Not long after the gates beneath the dreaded tower were swung open and a Luftwaffe Hauptmann in full uniform was ushered in. The relief felt by the men on seeing that uniform was almost tangible. The Hauptmann stood in front of the men, looked up at the leaden sky and grunted.

'Gentlemen,' he said. 'Please break your ranks and go back inside out of the rain.' The men could scarcely believe their ears. Civility—and from a German. They quickly scattered and made their way back into the shelter of the Effektenkammer, where the Hauptmann addressed them. It was like a dream to the men as he spoke in soft but precise terms. The Geneva Convention—Red Cross parcels—prisoner of war status—beds with sheets. He was describing things they had hardly dared to think about while in the Little Camp.

When the rain had eased the men were formed up once again to march out through the camp gates. As the steel barriers with their despised 'Jedem Das Seine' motto closed behind the airmen, not a single one of the 153 looked back as they marched along the Caracho Way, back to the railhead where by the ruins of the Gustloff Werke factories they boarded another goods train. They had left behind fourteen hospitalised members of their group, but were given assurances these men would not only be well treated, but transferred to their new camp once they were well. In fact the fourteen would receive absolutely no treatment at all, but as they recovered enough to leave Buchenwald they were packed off to join the others in their air force POW camp.

It was not a day entirely of celebration for the airmen. As well as the men in hospital they had also left behind Philip Hemmens, for whom the release from Buchenwald had come too late.

When they reached the waiting transport train their hopes sank somewhat as they noted the familiar '40 hommes/8 cheveaux' on the sides of the cattle trucks. But this time there was none of the appalling overcrowding they had endured on the inbound journey; the men were spread out over ten cars, with fresh straw on the floor, a stove, two guards, and an open door. It was almost first-class travel.

The men had not been told their ultimate destination, but were not unduly worried so long as it was far removed from the concentration camp. After a long wait the train finally pulled away from the station and built up speed as Buchenwald, its stink and its terror, receded in the distance.

* * *

Tom Malcolm was one of those left behind in Buchenwald. He was delirious with erysipelas in the camp hospital, a severe and highly contagious infection of the skin causing high fever and sometimes grave complications such as pneumonia and inflammation of the kidneys.

The potentially fatal malady could have been treated easily, and even eradicated, by the simple use of sulphonamides. But the disease was quite common in the hospital, where no medicines were dispensed, and Tom had to endure the most primitive of treatments—he was simply wrapped in wet blankets. It was a kill or cure method administered by indifferent attendants. Fortunately he survived and later joined the rest of the airmen in their POW camp, bunking in with Ray Perry and Jim Gwilliam, but any recollection of his latter days at Buchenwald are lost to him.

> To this day I have no memory of what happened to me during the time I was seriously ill in hospital, nor of my move across to the air force camp to join the others. What I do remember, quite vividly, is being cocooned for what seemed an eternity in sopping wet blankets.

Another of those too ill to be moved was Ed Carter-Edwards. He had developed pneumonia and pleurisy and was segregated with the other thirteen airmen who required medical treatment. The so-called hospital they occupied was Block 61, designated to hold the seriously ill and dying. It was a large hut, 25 metres long by 7 wide, holding nearly 800 patients from the Little Camp. It stank of death, putrefaction and defecation. Carter-Edwards was delirious for almost two weeks, his fever aggravated by the unsanitary conditions.

The only treatment he received was from a sympathetic inmate—a doctor and former professor from the University of Paris who managed to locate a syringe. At great personal risk he carefully inserted it into Ed's back, draining the fluid from his lungs. That was the only treatment Carter-Edwards was to receive for his illnesses. There was no medication, no aspirins, no antibiotics. The inmates either lived or died. If they survived they were lucky; if not, their corpse would be dragged out the next day. Some operations were performed by prison doctors on a table at one end of the hut. They were carried out in full view of the other patients, and were performed without any anaesthetic.

Every morning Russian prisoners would enter the hut and haul out those who had died during the night, sometimes as many as three dozen at a time. They would strip the bodies and write the deceased's name on his leg. Why they bothered to do this was a mystery to Ed, as the Russians were simply taking the corpses to the crematorium, but someone along the way must have entered the names in what would have been a very lengthy record book. The Russians piled the bodies on a homemade stretcher like cord-wood and bore them off. Some of the men suffered terribly before they died, crying out the names of loved ones, their bodies wracked with pain, their eyes rolling and their mouths gaping. They were dying in such numbers the Germans could not cremate the bodies fast enough.

The conditions were inhumane and the patients were that in name only. They had to sleep on a thin straw mattress without any blankets. Paper bandages were applied to open sores, but these were quickly eaten by the starving prisoners at the first opportunity. Every few days the Russians would be sent through with a hose to wash the whole place down—walls, floors and even patients in their beds—which surely hastened many a death. Dysentery was rife, and the resultant mess saturated the blankets, leaking through to those unfortunate enough to be on the bunk below. The Russians were brutal; they had no mercy for anyone, even though they knew many of those in the hut were their allies, and the patients were all treated in the same disgraceful manner. One can only assume that they were more concerned for their own survival.

Carter-Edwards' fellow patients lived and died in these terrible conditions and this time in the hut stands out most these days in his memories of Buchenwald. Death was all around him; he witnessed it, heard it, felt it, and came within a whisker of experiencing it.

After nearly six weeks in this death-house, Ed Carter-Edwards was considered well enough to be turned out, despite the fact that he was so weak he could barely stand, let alone walk. But with his release from that purgatory came the full realisation that he was essentially on his own—merely one of almost 40 000 doomed men whose sole preoccupation was survival as they shuffled aimlessly around the dusty compound, dazed and generally uncomprehending.

Two days after his release from the hut he was forced to work on a thriteen-kilometre railway line the Germans were laying outside the camp, working as part of a group for anything up to fourteen hours a shift. The original track, laid in mid-1943, ran down to Weimar with a 300-metre difference in elevation. He was made to labour, up to his knees in mud, in his debilitated condition. At one time he took it upon himself to complain to his guards. They merely laughed at the Canadian and one of them jerked his thumb towards the crematorium.

'You don't want to work?' he scoffed. 'Then perhaps you would prefer to report to the crematorium and go up the chimney?' Ed kept working.

The group dug an embankment, on top of which the guards stood, kicking stones and dirt down onto the workers to compound their misery in the cold, wet conditions. The Germans also had several guard dogs on long leashes, and they would gather up these leashes in their hands before advancing menacingly towards some terrified prisoner. They would then shout an order and partially release the leash. The dog would leap straight at the prisoner's face, and the guard's game was to see how close it came before the leash became taut and held the snapping beast at bay. The guards considered this a huge joke, and laughed at the misery of their victims.

Ed Carter-Edwards was eventually able to contact a friendly fellow prisoner by the name of Kurt Barrs, who had been training to be a doctor before joining the Dutch Underground. Barrs' work at the camp entailed keeping a headcount of the dead, and he somehow manipulated his lists to show that the Canadian had died. Barrs then told Ed to keep out of sight as much as possible, but there was no real need to hide in such a huge camp filled with so many similarly-dressed, emaciated people.

By this time Ed had been moved to the middle compound and by making discreet enquiries he found out, to his horror, that the rest of the airmen had been transferred to Stalag Luft III. He was now in a quandary. According to the records he was dead, and yet somehow he had to join his air force colleagues. he felt miserable, forgotten, and all alone.

He lived under terrible conditions, on a bed in a stack like baker's shelves. Each bed was nearly two metres wide, with four tiers against each wall, and the prisoners were jammed in like sardines. Movement was all but impossible. They slept in their clothes—the only clothes they had. There were no toilet facilities, no washroom and no soap, and Ed's discomfort was worsened by the fact that he couldn't speak the language of those around him.

Towards the end of November a German air force officer came into the camp and started asking after Carter-Edwards. He knew that Ed was still alive, so word had been smuggled out of the camp by someone, probably Kurt Barrs—Ed never did find out. Eventually news that he was being sought reached Ed, who decided to take a chance that the man was genuine. He surrendered to a guard and was taken immediately to the officer. With surprising swiftness he was taken under guard to Stalag Luft III, where he received an emotional welcome from the other airmen.

He found like at Sagan tough, with very little food and constant harassment from the Luftwaffe guards, but in his own words 'it was heaven compared to Buchenwald!'

7

Death March

With the warmth of a stove to comfort them, the rocking movement of the train and the hypnotic click-clacking as it moved over the rails, exhaustion soon took its toll on the group of airmen. Before too long they had all fallen into a deep, undisturbed sleep.

The following morning they were handed a large chunk of bread and a tough but palatable piece of sausage meat. A little later, after the train had stopped and the men had been permitted to relieve themselves by the rails, they were each given a mug of ersatz coffee.

With most of their earlier suspicions now gone, some of the men actually began to enjoy the ride, particularly as they could chatter freely. They even sang to express their feelings of relief. Jim Gwilliam remembers one of his guards as an elderly fellow from the Great War who was trying to play a mouth organ but only succeeding in making a woeful noise. Through gesticulation Jim asked if he might be able to have a go, and the guard handed over his instrument. Within seconds Jim had launched into a melancholy version of 'Lili Marlene' and the guard's face lit up with pleasure. Every time he tried to change the tune the guard would give him a pitiful look and beg him for another encore of what was obviously his favourite song. By the time they reached Sagan station at midday on the third day the guard had become friendly and was singing along with gusto. He and the other guards had given the prisoners some cigarettes, which they had all smoked together.

At Sagan the doors of the cattle trucks were rolled open to reveal an armed guard company dressed in the field blue of the Luftwaffe. Seeing these uniforms was a great relief for the airmen, many of whom had cringed on hearing the sudden blows on the door. The new guard company ordered the prisoners to detrain, and as they stood on the platform and stretched cramped limbs they looked around at the bordering pine forests. The misty morning air was sweet, clean and cool. Their former guards wished them all a sincere 'Guten abend!', following which the Luftwaffe detail marched the men uphill to their new camp, Stalag Luft III. The massive air force camp was sprawled over several hectares in a clearing hewn from the pines.

The men's reception at Sagan was overwhelming. The Luftwaffe authorities, who had no love for the SS and Gestapo, were genuinely shocked at their latest prisoners' condition. Once again the men were photographed and registered, given hot showers and kitted out with a complete airman's uniform and a set of underclothing, their first in months. To top it off they were each given an entire Red Cross parcel. They quickly withdrew to a quiet corner somewhere to examine the contents of their parcel in seclusion. Stanley Booker vividly recalls the ecstasy of having such luxury all to himself.

Needless to say it was quickly devoured, and many of us were violently sick shortly afterwards. At last we felt secure, into a proper organised routine, with the delight of a clean bunk with sheets and two clean blankets. However the greatest thrill was not the food, as relatively little as it was, but the sheer joy of being able to write that first Red Cross letter home, to hopefully let our loved ones know we were alive and well.

In the first edition of his later-revised book, *Escape From Germany* (Air Ministry Publication, 1956), Aiden Crawley made the following observations.

When [the prisoners] arrived the most distinctive sign of the treatment they had received was their shaved heads, but it was noticed on the first parade that as the German NCO who was counting the prisoners passed them they instinctively stiffened as if expecting a blow. A question they all asked the first day of their arrival was how many men went for the 'chop' each week. When their fellow prisoners did not understand they were surprised and explained that 'the chop' in Buchenwald meant execution... The story of Buchenwald and the other concentration camps is now well known. When these airmen first described what they had seen, the endless beatings, the starving and dying people lying on the floor in their own filth too weak to move, the stench, the lampshades made of human skin, the hospital where human beings were treated as guineapigs, their fellow prisoners found their story hard to believe.

One of the prisoners at Sagan, Kevin Murphy, told of his shock at the first sight of a friend, one of the Englishmen recently arrived from Buchenwald.

It was late October 1944 and the usual blanket of low cloud covered the pine trees that ringed Stalag Luft III. We no longer expected to be home for Christmas and were reconciling ourselves to yet another winter of wrestling with the weather and the 'goons'. I was walking with a friend around the 'circuit' that afternoon to keep warm and to pass the time until dinner, when I was accosted by a slight figure in a nondescript uniform. I stopped and looked uncertainly at this stranger who said, 'Don't you know me, Spud?' Peeling off the balaclava, he revealed a shaven head and a very pale face which I began to realise resembled an old friend, Ian Robb, a fellow navigator, missing presumed dead since August 1943! I was completely flabbergasted, but recovered enough to take him to my hut for a cup of Nescafé. There I presented him with a letter from his mother and his fiancee—his first news for eighteen months. We had a lot to say to each other. In addition to his obvious undernourishment he had lost the use of his left arm, having been operated upon for boils with a razor blade in Buchenwald. Fortunately Red Cross food and treatment by an Australian physiotherapist named Byrne restored him to the Ian I had known!

In late November word reached Stalag Luft III of the death of an airmen forced through illness to remain at Buchenwald. First Lieutenant Levitt Clinton Beck, a fighter pilot with the USAAF, had finally succumbed to purulent pleurisy.

Beck, a fresh-faced 24-year-old, had been born and raised for the first twelve years of his life in Houston, Texas. His family later moved to Huntington Park in California and on 23 March 1942 he enlisted in the Army Air Force at March Field, becoming an outstanding pilot on P-47 Thunderbolts. Shot down near Dreux in France on 29 June 1944, and while hiding out at a cafe in the little village of Anet, he began writing the outline of a book based on his experiences. Madame Mesnard, the sympathetic owner of the cafe, agreed to bury the completed and sealed manuscript under a shed behind the cafe until it could be retrieved after the war. In 1945 the manuscript was recovered as promised and later forwarded to Beck's parents by the Military Intelligence Office in Paris. It spoke of his youthful aspirations, his joy at being chosen as a pilot, and his plans once he got back to England. Verne and Levitt Beck Senior added the sad ending to the young American's story, and the manuscript was later published under the title *Fighter Pilot*, an absorbing book about a young man's experiences and thoughts on war.

Beck was one of those sold to the Germans by the traitor 'Captain Jacques', after hiding out in the notorious Piccadilly Hotel on the Boulevarde St Michel in Paris. An accomplished musician, Beck's cheerfulness and stoical defiance were an inspiration to others. While in Buchenwald he managed to obtain a tenor sax from a Green (criminal offender) prisoner and formed a small jazz trio, but the days and nights sleeping in wet clothes out in the open gave him pneumonia. He fought the disease, refusing to accept the dubious help offered by the camp infirmary. The rumoured news of the move to a regular POW camp gave Beck the strength to take his place at rollcalls, although he was growing weaker by the day. Finally his body could no longer support him and with the transfer a bare two days away he collapsed and was taken to the hospital where, as feared, he received no assistance or medication. Pleurisy set in, and his resistance weakened. He became delirious as a result of the beatings he had endured and the pain which now racked his body, but nothing was done to alleviate his suffering.

The day before Beck died, he sent a note to Joe Chopp from Antwerp, a trusted Belgian friend in the compound. In it he expressed the fear that he would never recover from his illness, and if the worst should occur he was to let Beck's parents know that his last thoughts were of them.

Levitt Beck slipped into the final oblivion on the evening of 29 November 1944. His body, like that of Philip Hemmens, was wheeled directly over to the crematorium and fed into one of the ovens. In a postwar letter to Beck's parents, fellow prisoner Donat Dauteuil remarked:

L.C. was one of the finest boys that I have had the pleasure of knowing. When our group of Allied prisoners at Buchenwald were in the lowest of spirits, L.C. was always there with some jazz to cheer us up. He had talked someone into getting him an old saxophone and he really knew how to put it to good use. He was always a source of good cheer and high spirits and, quite frankly, we all needed it at that time. His popularity was proven by the fact that 100 per cent of the original group were present at the Memorial Service which was held for him, when we learned of his death, at Stalag Luft III. Some of our best men stayed over there. Believe me when I say that your son was tops. A man to ride the river with.

On 12 January 1945 General Georgi Zhukov's Russian army group breached its bridgehead south of Warsaw on the upper Vistula and headed towards Silesia. To the north his armies crossed the Vistula from both sides of Warsaw, which fell on 17 January. Joseph Stalin had thrown 180 divisions into East Prussia and Poland alone, creating the greatest Russian offensive of the war. Fifteen days later the Russian advance had turned into an unstoppable tidal wave which swept all German resistance before it.

By now East and West Prussia had been cut off from the rest of the Reich, and General Zhukov triumphantly crossed the Oder near Lueben. In two weeks he had advanced 350 kilometres and reached German soil just 160 kilometres from Berlin. Shortly after General Dwight Eisenhower's 85 divisions began to close in on the Rhine, and by the end of February they had reached the river at several positions north of Dusseldorf, meeting rapidly diminishing resistance from the German forces.

According to Ray Perry, the consensus among the POWs at Sagan by 25 January was that they would soon be evacuated:

Rumours were rife around the camp that we were going to be moved towards the west. For those of us who had been in Fresnes prison, we wondered if we would be moved away from liberation again.

Although it was illegal to do so, many of us converted our kitbags to rucksacks by sewing on a pair of braces for straps. Being mid-winter and very cold, we knew we would want to carry as much clothing and food with us as possible—the Germans were by now so disorganised that we knew it would not be easy to survive any march in this weather. We were getting frequent falls of snow. Some of us thought that if the snow continued and froze we would be able to carry our gear easier if we made a sledge from a wooden box, with wooden runners fastened underneath.

On the morning of 27 January the prisoners' news service brought welcome tidings of Russian army advances less than 30 kilometres to the east, and the men hoped that the guards would move out and leave them to their eventual liberation. The rumbling thunder of Russian artillery attacking Breslau brought hope to the men, and created fearful anticipation amongst the Germans. The prisoners were placed on a one-hour standby to leave. Despite the freezing cold and sweeping snowstorms they moved amongst themselves out in the compound, talking over the prospect of freedom or evacuation. The men's kits and sledges were packed and ready for either event, and an air of nervous expectancy warmed the men despite the chill and whirling snow flakes.

At seven-thirty that evening the American Senior Officer of the camp's South compound was given 30 minutes to have his men at the front gate ready for evacuation. The POWs hurriedly donned their backpacks, tightened kits securely to their rough sledges (some of which had once been barracks doors) and formed up in lines at the gate according to their blocks. The wind whipped at their faces but the men waited pensively, wondering what fate lay beyond the familiar wire gates. Then the gates swung open and they were on the move.

The West and Centre compounds were given their marching orders shortly after and the camp began to empty rapidly. The remainder of the men cooked and ate the biggest meal they could manage but still had to leave precious food behind, unable to fit it into their kitbags or knapsacks. Next to be called out were the prisoners from the North and Belaria compounds, and they tagged onto the long string of apprehensive marchers filing out into the countryside.

At 8.45 p.m. orders came through for the last of the prisoners, those from East compound, to prepare for immediate evacuation. Time dragged on as delay followed delay, and the fully clothed men dozed off in their barracks as they waited. Finally, at six the following morning, the men were ordered to line up outside their blocks. Ninety minutes later on Sunday, 28 January, the last of the POWs steadily moved out of the East compound, becoming the last Allied servicemen to evacuate Stalag Luft III. Even though few guards remained behind at this time the Senior British Officer ordered the men not to make any escape attempts. It was essential that they stay together, not only for mutual support and assistance, but because the murder of 50 officers from the camp following the ill-fated Great Escape ten months earlier was still fresh in the minds of the long-term Sagan residents. Ray Perry, one of the last to leave, describes the final minutes of the evacuation:

> It was snowing lightly over the camp. We moved towards the Red Cross store to get a parcel each, which I stacked on my sledge and, as we were

the last, we started throwing some parcels over the fence to some Russian prisoners in a nearby compound. There was still quite a bit left in the store when we moved out.

A weak dawn had begun to streak the eastern horizon as they pulled out, at the end of a long centipede line stretching more than twelve kilometres. The road, originally covered with 20 centimetres of snow, was now just a muddy quagmire bordered by metre-high snow drifts. The men were wearing every available piece of clothing and carrying as much kit and food as they could. Every hundred metres or so along the column trudged the unhappy guards, machine-guns at the ready.

With the Russian and Allied armies now exerting the squeeze on Germany from two fronts the prisoners were forced in a meandering westerly direction. They slept in barns, open fields, churches and schools. They bartered for bread with German people along the way, using cigarettes as currency. They endured freezing winds and blizzards. Many died from a combination of exposure and exhaustion, and others, worst of all, as a result of ground strafing by Allied aircraft. The roadsides became littered with kit items and even food as the weary marchers found their loads too heavy to bear. Precious diaries and treasured souvenirs were discarded by desperate men whose sole thought was survival and trodden into the slush by those who followed. The distances they travelled varied between 20 and 30 kilometres daily.

At Spremburg, a railhead between Muscau and Cottbus, the long column was split in two and the prisoners taken in different directions. Some moved south-west to Moosburg, while others were marched north-westward to keep ahead of the rapid Russian push. The route was eventually diverted eastwards—this time to avoid the oncoming British forces. Hundreds of marchers were herded off to the former naval prison camp of Marlag-Milag near Bremen, while others were entrained for a one day journey to Stalag IIIA at Luckenwalde.

Suddenly it was all over. The victorious Russian, British and American forces finally overwhelmed the remaining pockets of German resistance, liberating many thousands of exhausted but exultant POWs. For those whose freedom came at the hands of the Russians, however, the last lap home was held up for several weeks. Negotiations between the Americans and the stubborn Russians delayed their final release and the war was over before many of them planted their feet on British soil once again.

Back in England the men were given a quick delousing, an advance in pay (one pound for officers, ten bob for NCOs), blank telegram forms with which to notify their next of kin they were safe, some clothing and food coupons. For many their first meal back home was an occasion—the culmination of months and even years of starvation. Before being allowed to return to their homes many headed off into nearby towns and villages to fulfil some long-held dreams, and to eat the fish and chips they had talked of so lovingly and longingly as a prisoner of war, smothered in salt and vinegar, and washed down with a pint from the local pub. This, more than anything else, made them feel they were finally home, and free men once more.

*　　*　　*

Buchenwald concentration camp remained in operation for only six months following the departure of the bulk of the airmen. The story of its fall only became known to them after their return to England.

In mid-1943 an International Camp Committee had been formed in Buchenwald, the main purpose of which was to coordinate military and sabotage operations by all nationalities represented in the camp. The men of these nations, particularly the powerful German Communists, finally came to an agreement over such activities and began to work in concert. The resultant acts of resistance and covert operations worked far more smoothly. The ICC provided a common front of all inmates prepared to work against the SS, to build evidence against traitors, and to arm themselves for self-preservation in the event of German treachery at the time of liberation.

Countries represented at frequent secret meetings included Germany, Russia, France, Italy, Austria, the Netherlands, Czechoslovakia, Yugoslavia, Poland and Belgium, and the absolute authority of the ICC was respected by all nationalities. Meetings were held in the camp hospital, while trusted inmates provided the necessary security lookouts.

Several radio receivers were hidden within the huts, and broadcasts were carefully monitored and transcribed. By March 1945 three transmitters had also been constructed in Buchenwald, but due to the high risks involved had not been operated. None of the hidden radio receivers or transmitters was ever discovered by the Germans.

It is astonishing to note that by the spring of 1945 the resistance movement within Buchenwald possessed a vast array of weapons. These had either been smuggled into the camp or manufactured within it.

The remarkable inventory listed one light machine-gun, 96 rifles and a similar number of pistols, 16 hand grenades, 107 camp-made grenades, 1100 petrol incendiary bombs and about 50 hand-made knives, slashing weapons and bludgeons.

Secret training in the use of firearms and grenades was carried out in a disinfection room. Other prisoners had discovered the means by which they could shut off power to the electrified fence, and wooden planks were prepared in the event the gates had to be stormed.

On Wednesday evening, 4 April 1945, Kommandant Pister ordered his guard company to commence the immediate and total evacuation of the 8000 Jews still remaining in the camp. These Jews were told to present themselves for rollcall, but none obeyed. They stayed defiantly in their huts knowing that evacuation would mean almost certain death. Meanwhile the leaders of the camp resistance decided to bring delaying tactics into effect at the massive rollcall, which caused its postponement by the SS until the following day. By this time, and according to the scheme, the Jews had intermingled with the Aryans, destroyed all personal means of identification, and removed the hated yellow stars from their sleeves.

The next day the guards began to hunt out the Jews, but their task was a difficult one for all 8000 of them were spread throughout the camp. Sporadic shooting rang out during the day. Eventually 1500 of the Jews had been rounded up and were forced to evacuate the camp under guard. The fears of these men were later realised; hundreds died or were murdered during the forced march that followed.

That same day, 5 April, Christopher Burney and his three surviving SOE colleagues, Southgate and the Newton brothers, received reliable information that they were about to be seized by the SS. Before they could be taken the four men were hidden in a cramped cellar less than a metre high beneath Hut 56 in the Little Camp.

With extraordinary confusion occurring outside the Little Camp the following day, and with most of the SS concentrating on the Jewish evacuation, Burney and his companions felt it safe enough to leave their tiny hiding place and mingle with the other prisoners. They returned to their cellar that night and towards ten o'clock word reached them that the Gestapo had presented a list of 47 names to the SS, with orders for their immediate execution. The ICC spy system was now operating so efficiently that the list of names became available to the conspirators eight hours before the SS could act upon it, and the men named in the list were hurriedly moved into the cellar. The four SOE men felt it safe enough for them to return to Block 50. During the night they learned that another 8000 men, those the Germans regarded as the worst troublemakers in the camp, were to be evacuated and transported to the concentration camps at Flossenberg, Dachau, and Theresienstadt in Czechoslovakia. This was carried out on 7 April.

The next day, with American fighter planes roaming openly across the skies and land forces just twelve kilometres away, Kommandant Pister announced that the entire camp was to be evacuated by the following Monday, and that 10 000 inmates were to leave immediately. Using a hidden radio transmitter installed in the camp cinema, a Polish member of the ICC named Gwidon Damazyn transmitted a message in morse intended for General George Patton, using the 36.8m wavelength identified to the operators by the Allied airmen. The message, sent in both English and German, was received by the American forces and acknowledged, with an added assurance that the camp's liberation was at hand. This promise of freedom was short-lived for many, as the Germans successfully evacuated half of the remaining inmates—Russians, Czechs, Poles, and Frenchmen. Despite this massive drain of prisoners, over 20 000 of them still remained in Buchenwald.

On Wednesday 11 April the camp defence force readied itself to take over the guard company. By now most of the SS contingent had either left with the other prisoners or in their own transport. An eerie silence reigned throughout the camp; there was no shooting, and very few guards had been left in attendance. Confusion was rampant. The Kommandant was clearly in a quandary, knowing that the Allied tanks were near, but not wishing to relinquish his control over Buchenwald. Prisoner lists and orders had either been destroyed or diverted by the camp insurgents, and false orders were finding their way into Pister's office. Matters were not aided by the constant wailing of air-raid sirens and the desertion of many of his guards into the woods. The SS had absconded with half of the camp's food supplies, leaving the remaining prisoners with a meagre 250 grammes of bread apiece.

The Leipzig-Halle-Magdeberg area had been given a fearful pasting by Allied bombers and fighters and the prisoners knew the end, whatever it might bring, was near. It was rumoured, apparently with some foundation, that a squad of SS troops armed with flamethrowers had arrived at Weimar with orders to burn the camp and incinerate the remaining inmates. They were to be aided in this gruesome task by a large squad of Hitler Youth who were to take control of the camp, thus releasing the guard company for urgent combat assignments. Fortunately the SS death squad moved out of Weimar in the face of the American advance, and the train transporting the Hitler Youth unit was captured.

Pister finally admitted defeat and fled the camp. He was arrested after the war and placed on trial in April 1947 at Dachau, where he was sentenced to death and hanged.

Gunfire could be heard in the woods outside the camp and the prisoners could see long convoys of German artillery and lines of soldiers evacuating the area. Very few guards now remained at their posts, and the united camp defence forces decided that the time was ripe to take over control of Buchenwald.

At 2.30 p.m., brandishing guns, grenades and makeshift weapons, the prisoners' defence force stormed out of their huts in rapidly swelling numbers. Witnessing this uprising the few remaining guards clambered out of their towers and fled. Within the hour a huge white flag, hoisted on the mast above the main tower, was flapping triumphantly in the breeze. The victorious prisoners had captured 220 of their former guard company and seized nearly a thousand rifles. Guns were fired into the air and men went berserk in a delirium of freedom, cutting the barbed wire fences, breaking into German offices, and generally running amok after years of confinement and the ever-present spectre of death.

As five o'clock neared the din in the camp suddenly died and the men's voices became hushed as a heavy clanking noise could be heard approaching along the road. Then a huge cheer went up as the first of several American tanks roared into the camp compound and hundreds of enraptured men swarmed their way, striving to touch these imperious machines and greet their liberators.

The Americans, for their part, were appalled at the ghastly scene confronting them. They had already driven past countless hundreds of bodies in the Weimar woods, where groups of evacuees had been massacred, but none of them was ready for the massive wave of hysterical living skeletons surging towards them. Shock followed shock for the Americans as they moved further into the camp. Beyond the filthy hordes of emaciated survivors were the corpses, piled haphazardly in mountains of putrefying flesh. It was a sight none of them would ever forget. Gone was the sensation of triumph, to be replaced by despair and a rage beyond comprehension. Having tasted the sweetness of a hard-fought victory over the might of Hitler's Third Reich, they were hardly ready for the grim legacy of his vicious doctrines.

The battle for Weimar was not fully resolved at this time, and to the dismay of the camp inmates the tanks were forced to withdraw temporarily. The Germans had launched a last-ditch counter-offensive in the area and Buchenwald was right in the middle of the battle.

For hours the shells roared overhead from both sides, several landing in the camp itself. The terrified prisoners lay on the floor of their huts or out in the compound, hands clasped over their heads in fear. After what seemed an eternity, the Americans secured the area. Once again the tanks rolled into the camp.

Buchenwald concentration camp was officially liberated on 12 April 1945, and teams of military doctors and nurses moved in to tend the sick and dying. Unbelieving inmates were given food and clothing, cigarettes, sweets, and other small luxuries. A sad after-effect of this kindness was that many prisoners died from a diet too-rich after years of bland food. Their stomachs just could not cope.

For Americans involved in the military operation, that momentous 12 April would come to mean more than the occasion on which they freed the inhabitants of a notorious death camp. Their triumph was quickly tempered by the devastating news from home that their beloved President, Franklin Roosevelt, had died.

Following their liberation the former inmates broke into the German storehouses and helped themselves to provisions long denied. The Americans, appalled at the magnitude of the German atrocities, initially turned a blind eye to several acts of revenge carried out by uncontrollable prisoners who had lost friends and loved ones to the followers of the Nazi doctines. The day after the second liberation they reluctantly took steps to prevent the Germans from being attacked by the vengeance-seeking prisoners. Nevertheless the Russian prisoners of war wanted revenge, so they commandeered as many vehicles as possible and sped off in the direction of Weimar, seeking out victims.

At the behest of General Dwight Eisenhower, a British Parliamentary delegation left London bound for Weimar on the afternoon of Friday, 20 April, in order 'that they may themselves have ocular and first-hand proof of these atrocities'. They arrived at Buchenwald the following day, toured such areas as the mortuary and crematorium, saw the rotting heaps of emaciated corpses awaiting a more dignified funeral, and talked with many of the inmates. Extracts from their subsequent report reflect the difficulty they had in coming to terms with the terrible inhumanities perpetrated at the camp.

A detailed report presented to us by representatives of an anti-Fascist committee stated that, up to 1st April, the total number of those who had died or been killed at Buchenwald, or immediately on removal therefrom to subsidiary 'extermination camps' was 51 572—at least 17 000 of them since 1st January, 1945. The camp has now been thrown open, and a certain number of its inmates must have left independently. Detailed camp records, including nominal rolls, were left behind by the Nazis; but, at the time of our visit, it had not been possible to start drawing up rolls of those still in the camp, the American medical and sanitary authorities being naturally preoccupied with the cleaning of the camp (a task performed partly by German civilians from the neighbourhood, parties of whom are also brought daily to see what had been done in their name and in their midst), and with problems of feeding and medical attention.

Although the work of cleaning the camp had gone on busily for over a week before our visit, and conditions must therefore have been improved considerably, our immediate and continuing impression was of intense general squalor; the odour of dissolution and disease still pervaded the entire place. One of the first of a number of huts that we entered was one of the best; it was divided into small rooms with cement floor and windows, four of which had been used, the American authorities informed us, as a brothel to which the higher-grade prisoners—those employed in various supervisory jobs, with extra rations and other privileges—were allowed to resort for 20 minutes at a time. When the Americans arrived, fifteen women were found in this brothel. This hut was one of those now used as transit hospitals for some of the worst cases of malnutrition. Many were unable to speak; they lay in a semi-coma, or following us with their eyes. Others spoke freely, displaying sores and severe scars and bruises which could have been caused by kicks or blows. They lay on the floor and under quilts. All of them were in a state of extreme emaciation. We were told by the U.S. authorities that, since their arrival, the number of deaths had been reduced from about a hundred a day to 35 on the day before our visit.

One half-naked skeleton, tottering painfully along the passage as though on stilts, drew himself up when he saw our party, smiled and saluted.

In preparing this report, we have endeavoured to write with restraint and objectivity, and to avoid obtruding personal reactions or emotional comments. We would conclude, however, by stating that it is our considered and unanimous opinion, on the evidence available to us, that a policy of steady starvation and inhuman brutality was carried out at Buchenwald for a long period of time; and that such camps as this mark the lowest point of degradation to which humanity has yet descended. The memory of what we saw and heard at Buchenwald will haunt us ineffaceably for many years.

On 11 April 1947, two years to the day after Patton's victorious Third Army had stormed into Buchenwald, 31 defendants from the former concentration camp were brought before an American war crimes trial convened at Dachau. Prosecutors at the trial charged the male and female defendants with responsibility for the deaths of 53 000 inmates and the torturing of thousands of others. All 31 were eventually convicted of violating the laws and usage of war by their systematic cruelties and mass murders. A total of 22 were sentenced to hang, five including Ilse Koch were sentenced to life imprisonment, one to 20 years, two to 15 years and one to 10 years.

Among those receiving the death penalty were the last Kommandant, Hermann Pister, and Max Schobert, the former camp leader. Included in those given life sentences were Frau Ilsa Koch, and Prince Josias zu Waldeck, a confidant of Hitler and first German of royal blood to be tried for war crimes. Edwin Katzen-Ellenbogen, 64, a former resident of the United States and one of the camp physicians, was another given a life sentence. He had started out as a Buchenwald prisoner, but later opted to aid his Nazi captors.

On 3 May 1944 a fourteen-year-old Jewish girl named Anne Frank, who was to die at Auschwitz the following year, penned a few words on the appalling and disastrous effects of totalitarianism in her secret but subsequently famous diary while hiding from the Nazis with her family in Amsterdam. Her simple, innocent words reflect on the cruelty of those times.

I don't believe that the big men, the politicians and the capitalists alone are guilty of the war. Oh no, the little man is just as keen, otherwise the

155

people of the world would have risen in revolt long ago! There is an urge and rage in people to destroy, to kill, to murder, and until all mankind, without exception, undergoes a great change, wars will be waged, everything that has been built up, cultivated and grown, will be destroyed and disfigured, after which mankind will have to begin all over again.

*　*　*

The eventual return to the comfort of their homes and families did not bring about an end to the conflict for many of the KLB airmen. Within the home environment the mental scars of Buchenwald which went unnoticed and certainly unheeded as prisoners came as a shock to the men's wives and close friends. The ghosts of the past would reach out to haunt them for the rest of their lives, and the fears they brought home were to manifest themselves in many different ways and to varying degrees.

Even today, after 50 years, painful memories of the past still lurk within many of these men, occasionally rising to the surface when a familiar sight, sound or experience opens an unwanted door to the past. The sound of someone speaking German, or a child screaming, can create nervous distress in them, or they become fretful when evocative images appear on their television screen. It is an inescapable facet of their lives.

The majority of the Australian and New Zealand airman have confessed to their own postwar traumas, but for Mervyn Fairclough there was little doubt that the tentacles of black horror reached out for him after the war, taking him inexorably back to the hell camp. Despair would finally claim him as a victim, and cause his premature death at the relatively youthful age of 40.

Returning to Australia outwardly fit and well, Mervyn Fairclough resumed life on the farm at Dumbleyung with his wife Elaine and baby son Brian. The young West Australian didn't talk much about his war experiences, and even now his widow only knows the barest of details concerning his capture and imprisonment. He preferred to keep his memories to himself—a silence Elaine respected, but tried hard to understand. She knew he had lived through quite severe traumas in France and Germany, but to all intents and purposes they had resumed their married life together, and there was great joy when Rhonda was born in 1946.

Curiously, it was an act of official courtesy two years after his return that caused the first visible disturbance in the gentle, doting father. That day a card arrived from the local post office, advising him of a parcel to be collected. He claimed the small package, which contained a familiar gold ring and a letter. The ring, inscribed with his and Elaine's names, was the one which had been torn so violently from his finger by the guard at Fresnes prison. An accompanying note from the American Embassy informed him that the ring had been found amongst the thousands of effects abandoned by the Germans when they were swept from Paris, and Fairclough's name and address had finally been located in the records.

He stuck the ring in his pocket and never mentioned it at home, although Elaine noticed he had become more pensive, and she would often see him looking at the ring, obviously brooding over the past.

The next jolt came when they decided to take in a movie. The feature film that night happened to be *Odette*, a black and white movie based on the wartime experiences of Odette Samson, the SOE agent parachuted into France who was later captured and brutally tortured by the Gestapo at Fresnes prison. Mervyn Fairclough watched the movie in complete silence until the setting changed to the corridors of Fresnes prison. A sudden panic overwhelmed him as he sat there, seeing once again the familiar passageways and cells. Then, almost hysterical, he leapt to his feet and cried, 'No, no! I've been there! I've been there!' He left the theatre a badly shaken man.

The nightmares came more frequently to him after this, mostly dreams of being blown out of his aircraft, the savage beatings, and the inhumanities he had witnessed. In his late thirties the former airman, whose children remember him as a caring and interested parent, took to rambling on about the strangest subjects. He destroyed and discarded almost everything pertaining to his war service.

One Saturday in late 1963 he went to see his son Brian play football for Claremont League in Perth. Although he was not feeling well he would not miss the pride he always felt in watching his son take the field. At home, Elaine was doing some housework as she listened to a live broadcast of the match. Suddenly the radio announcer reported that a spectator had collapsed in the Member's Stand and was being taken away by ambulance. Elaine's blood ran cold. Instinctively she knew it was Mervyn, and this was confirmed just two hours later when a staff member from the Royal Perth Hospital rang to say that her husband was in Casualty with a severe heart condition. Brian drove to Perth, only to find his father standing stubbornly on the footpath, demanding to be taken home. Fortunately he allowed himself to be taken inside for treatment, but when he came home he had lost any inclination to work on the farm again. Physically he was in reasonable shape, but his nerves were shattered by the chronic nightmares. After this he was in and out of the local hospital at Katanning, and Hollywood Repatriation in Perth.

Near the end, when he was home he would often be found wandering around outside the house at night, and Elaine would quietly watch over him until he returned to bed. Sometimes he would grab her shoulder and shake her, asking who she was, and then his mind would wander and he would babble on about having to get away from the Russians. Mervyn knew there was something terribly wrong with his mind, and in his less-frequent lucid times he would plead with Elaine, 'Don't let the children see me like this!'

Finally, on Thursday 23 July 1964, a specialist from the Repatriation Hospital called Elaine in and explained that it would be better all round if her husband was given specialist care in the hospital. He added that intense psychological help was needed. Returning home, Elaine put all their affairs in order prior to Mervyn's admittance. While waiting for the specialist to call back with an admission date she tended her husband at the local Katanning Hospital. Then a week later, and without warning, Mervyn Fairclough died. His end was quick and peaceful.

He had been an active young man, a man who loved his wife and children, and he had experienced the wonderment of holding his first grandchild. But there was little doubt that his experiences in Fresnes and Buchenwald had unhinged a corner of his mind, almost indiscernibly to begin with, but in the end consuming him until he could no longer cope with living or life.

Following her husband's death, Elaine Fairclough became deeply involved in charity work, and in 1985 was awarded the Order of Australia, of which she is justly proud.

★ ★ ★

And what of the other KLB men today? While many are loath to reflect on those days, and with good reason, others such as Ian Robb, from Chalfont St Giles in Buckinghamshire, have volunteered the following candid comments:

Those of us who survived the experiences of living with the Resistance of all nationalities, Fresnes prison and Buchenwald, and who incurred no physical or mental disability were in fact privileged. That may seem an odd statement, but we saw men and women prepared to risk prison and even death to help those who were complete strangers with the sole purpose of ridding their country of the invader, and displaying cool courage of the highest order.

On the other hand, we witnessed the real horror and brutality of Nazi tyranny. Despite all the reports in newspapers and books, on film, television and radio, I believe the scale of the Holocaust was such as to make it impossible for those who did not experience it to comprehend the full horror. We who did have no doubts that, despite all the suffering and loss of life, there was no alternative but to fight the war to the bitter end, and to make sure we are never again left defenceless and at the mercy of other aggressors.

Ed Carter-Edwards from Hamilton, Ontario, was shot down on 7 June 1944 while acting as a wireless operator/air gunner with No.427 Squadron, RCAF. He too described the lingering aftershocks of his days in the concentration camp:

After I got home, I still suffered the effects of Buchenwald and had to receive help at a convalescent hospital in Ancaster. I was there about three months and finally got straightened out and went back to work.

Luckily the years have cast some shadows over my mind, blacking out much of the Buchenwald experience. But the mental pictures remain, and are sometimes triggered easily by a war movie or if I hear a German accent, or even a siren or planes flying overhead. These things are not as bad as they used to be, but they are still there. I'm very happy to have survived but I still feel that it should never have happened. Not only that I shouldn't have suffered all those inhumanities and indignities, but also that for a nation, even a nation like Germany, it was totally wrong to develop the camps. What purpose did they serve other than to cause suffering and indignity to human beings? I'm sure men and women deserve more than that, no matter what nationality they are and under what circumstances. These circumstances of degradation are totally unnecessary in the twentieth century. It's the one thing that will live with me and die with me.

I have great difficulty now warming to any Germans; no matter how

159

friendly they are or how far removed from the scene. They are still basically of that heritage; it's happened once, it's happened twice, and it could happen again—and this is one of the things I fear.

Bill Gibson of Halifax, Nova Scotia, a Canadian rear gunner on a Lancaster shot down on 4 July 1944, also spoke openly of the anguish he still feels:

I'm terrified of dying . . . we saw death in some horrible ways [and] these things frighten me. In the first year I was home I could not sleep without a light on [and] every morning I'm scared when I wake up. I know another chap who tells me it's in the afternoon he's scared. I think we all of us have a psychiatric reaction to those years. I have found, and other people have found, that it's difficult to have people believe you; that you were there and those things happened.

Under an agreement signed with West Germany in June 1964, one million pounds became available to British victims of Nazi persecution. The British KLB airmen received a basic compensation payment of £183.50 for the time they spent in Buchenwald. Some of the former airmen gave media interviews at the time and many, including Bob Harper of Warrington, Lancashire, were critical of the payment:

I was an RAF warrant officer flying as an observer and I was shot down over France in November 1943. I was with the Resistance for six weeks and then I was picked up by the Gestapo. I was in three different French prisons for about ten months. Later I was sent to Buchenwald and spent three months there before going to a prison camp. I don't get any compensation for the months I was imprisoned by the Gestapo. The £184 is for the time in Buchenwald. I think it's shocking. It's as if the Foreign Office has allowed the Germans to put us off with a token payment.

Londoner George Watmough's weight fell from 80 to 37 kilograms in Buchenwald:

Fortunately I was sent to a prisoner of war camp after three months in Buchenwald. I'm not bitter about the scale of the compensation. After all these years I didn't really expect to get anything, but I can see why some of the former prisoners are disappointed. I'm lucky—my health wasn't affected so badly, but when you think of it, £2 a day isn't much for being in Buchenwald.

John Clark from Leicestershire was able to receive a little more money from the compensation fund:

I was in Buchenwald for three months and doctors say my health is permanently affected. It seems I had TB when I was in the camp. Even now if I get a cold I just collapse. I've had more from the fund than many of the others. I've had £1100, but I think this may be because I've never had any disability allowance. Compared with some of the other lads in Buchenwald, I've been lucky!

From his cosy home in Victoria, British Columbia, Art Kinnis recently told the author of the problems faced by many of his KLB friends over the past five decades:

The fact that no one knew where we were was always in our thoughts. We existed, and those who could block out their surroundings fared better than those who couldn't. To this day much that happened has become hidden in our minds, and now can only be recalled with difficulty. After we were released, and for many months, nightmares and sleepless nights were our constant lot. Some required more help than others, but we're all aware of the enormous help our wives gave us. Every man amongst us will be grateful to his wife till the day he dies for the moral and spiritual help they gave us when we returned home confused, angry, and filled with the terrors of that place. We truly bless them one and all.

Nervous breakdowns were not uncommon. It has only been over recent years that we have been able to resurrect some of the happenings to our sympathetic friends and those who were there. It was something of the past that we were afraid to disturb because of the consequences that might result.

Chest conditions, sinus and other problems that started then are still with us, and many still show the scars of the bedbugs. The mental scars do not show, but they're like that part of an iceberg which lays below the surface. Some have required medication and psychiatric help for extended periods.

Former KLB Senior Officer Phil Lamason remains proud of the men under his command at Buchenwald:

I haven't talked very much about my experiences during the war. No, I've hardly mentioned it since. But although we witnessed some particularly horrible things New Zealand is a long way from Germany, and Malcolm Cullen is the only chap here from those days, and he lives some distance away from me. Apart from my family, people don't know of my involvement in these things, although I suppose I gained a little notoriety in Bruce Marshall's book, *The White Rabbit*. Sure there are the nightmares, but not many at all now, and in any case I'm a light sleeper. If little else, I suppose my experiences made me far more tolerant in many ways and not quite as dogmatic, but then we all naturally mellow over the years.

I hold no particular grudges from those days, but I still find it quite unbelievable that a civilised race like the Germans could behave in such a manner. I found them to be a very disciplined people who, if they're told to do something, will do it. He mightn't like it, but he'll do it. What they did was inexcusable, whatever their philosophies, and far too horrible to ever describe. I'm sorry, but it was something you had to see—you had to have been there to have any sort of comprehension of the gross atrocities they went on with, day after day.

Following my eventual liberation and return to England, I was asked to consider commanding one of the Okinawa squadrons for the final attack on Japan, but the New Zealand Air Force said no, I was to return home. In fact I arrived back in New Zealand the day after they dropped the bomb on Hiroshima, so the war was all but over, and I returned to the land.

Through this book, I'd like to pay tribute to the entire group of fellow airmen in Buchenwald. They were from different countries, living together in one of the most horrific places on God's earth, but to a man they gave me their unquestioning loyalty, which meant a lot to me at the time. If there is any singularly good recollection of those days then that is it. They were, and are, a tremendous group of men, and I feel deeply honoured to have been their Senior Officer during that period.

8

Man of a Ghost

Stanley Booker, MBE, from Bracknell in Berkshire was one of the English contingent in Buchenwald, and he undertook a pilgrimage with his wife to the site of the notorious camp in September 1984. They returned in April 1985 to commemorate the fortieth anniversary of the liberation of Buchenwald.

Stan Booker was the sole British representative, and his homage to his fellow airmen, and the SOE group, is gratefully recorded as a fitting finale and tribute to those who endured and died within the barbed wire of Buchenwald. His words were written prior to the fall of the Berlin Wall and the unification of Germany, when movement around the German Democratic Republic, or East Germany, was certainly restricted, but could be achieved with a little patience.

'At the Hotel Elephant in Weimar we were made genuinely welcome, especially when they learned that I had been a former guest up on the hill all those years before. Weimar itself has a cultural link with the past, and the classics (Goethe and others dominate the place), but they have not tried to hide the grimmer association with its more evil past. There are conspicuous signposts indicating the route to the Nationale Mahn und Gedenkstatte, Buchenwald, and a regular bus for visitors runs from the main railway station. However, on the day we made the visit there were a series of roadblocks which made the route rather vague and confusing. Being a very large Soviet garrison town, with numerous bustling army barracks very much in prominence, I had no wish to loiter too much, so I used my navigator's natural instinct and headed for the main station. I reasoned that during the war we had set off from there to mount the steep wooded hill the five or six miles to the camp, so the obvious thing would be to find the route of the rail spur, which we eventually did. Although the track had been lifted, there was no problem in taking the road through the culvert, and after climbing up through the lovely beech woods we came out onto the site of the former Gustloff Werke, and the shabby old railhead, and the platforms that had struck so much terror into so many thousands of hapless souls in the past.

Following the route of the old 'Road of Blood', the Caracho Way, we came upon the five large multi-storied brick barrack blocks that were the former SS Headquarters on the southern perimeter track, and which are now used as administration offices and a tourist hotel/restaurant for the many thousands of visitors they have from all over the world. Out of politeness, not having written to say we were coming, we reported to the Reception Centre, asking for the Museum Director, Dr Trostorff, who was unfortunately away in Moscow on a conference. We were greeted, almost overwhelmed by Herr Rothmann, the Deputy Director, who was very moved to meet us, and settle us in to what he appreciated could be quite a traumatic occasion. He immediately cancelled all his engagements for the day, giving us his complete personal attention. There were a million things to talk about; fortunately I speak fair German.

Being the first former British prisoner, and having read a personal account that I had submitted to the Museum, we almost seemed like old friends—not at all the reception I had somehow expected, for the hurt, even after all these years, had never healed, and I think somehow, perhaps because we were behind the Curtain, I didn't appreciate what a common bond of understanding there was.

We seemed to talk about everything, and time was going too fast— it all seemed unreal; there we were, in the former dreaded SS Kommandant's office—SS Sturmbahnfuhrer Koch and his equally infamous successor, Pister, who was in charge during our sojourn there. We were taken to the briefing room where there was a vast scaled model of the former camp, on which every feature suddenly became real, and moved on down through the remarkably well preserved and original SS buildings until we came up to the gateway—the entrance to the former camp. The camp remained, preserved, just as it was when functioning at the close of the Second World War. The clock over the gateway was stopped at 3.15 p.m.—the time the white flag went up and the camp freed itself from the yoke of the SS tyrants, back on the 11th of April, 1945.

The electrified perimeter wire, the raised guard towers surmounting the fence, the evil crematorium (no longer belching out its foul smoke), were all completely intact and preserved for visitors to examine, even to the complete gas ovens, the furnaces, the gallows and the lethal syringes. The conspicuous main entrance, with adjoining dark and fearful bunker cells were open for inspection. All that was missing were the row upon row of the long low huts that were packed in the space between the perimeter wires—they were burned for sanitary reasons after the war, but their foundations are there, calling out to be seen in their geometrically precise rows, grim reminders of their former function.

Beyond the crematorium was the huge three-storied Effekten-kammer, now the new museum, alongside of which was the low reception building where the induction process took place—the showers and the barbers with their electric clippers and the mountains of hair. On the horizon, beyond the wire, was a wired gate—the entrance to our own private hell—the former Little Camp, now mercifully returned to nature. Beyond the former 'Kanteen' building, now used as a cultural centre, was the dreaded quarry. Taking the narrow path down into its depths was like treading on hallowed ground—oh, the ghosts that must have been close to me, now so silent and still, but sending that shiver down one's spine at the terrible events only history can preserve.

Passing through the gates into the former camp was perhaps one of the most traumatic moments I have ever experienced. There was such a vast contrast between the lovely natural woodlands, the proud beeches that surround the outer perimeter fence. Within, everything was so utterly stark and barren. It was so still, so quiet, so completely lifeless; no birds sang, not a blade of grass—it was as if nature had turned its back on the evil establishment as its own form of protest. I uttered a silent prayer that I had been spared the cruel fate that had befallen so many thousands of those nameless inmates who never lived to see their loved ones, their homes and freedom.

As you would expect from a German national memorial, this once infamous establishment is very well organised and most efficiently run. Quite unbelievably everything is intact—there has been no vandalism—the place is not guarded in any way, and visitors can come and go just as they please without any control of entry or restriction. There are no police or uniforms of any kind, except the occasional visiting Soviet soldier wandering around the various internal features, all of which, not unnaturally, carry display signs in both Russian and German. At various main features there are guides who remain discreetly in the background, but who carry lingophones, giving helpful commentaries and assistance when required.

The day we were there, there were very few visitors, but those who were walked almost with reverence, and spoke in low voices as if in a church. Later, parties of school children arrived, aged between twelve and fourteen, accompanied by their elderly school teachers. Apparently, in the GDR, every school child at a certain age has to attend one or other of the former concentration camps, now established as national memorials (Buchenwald, Sachsenhausen and Ravensbruck) for a full day of indoctrination. They are given a series of lectures, shown films and given conducted tours of the entire encampments and the respective museums. Nothing is held back; they receive the full treatment of the evil of the Nazi dynasty and how the camps were run.

Within the main camp area, on the site of the former Block 17 (where the few Allied SOE inmates were housed), there is a simple stone slab, commemorating the murder of the Allied parachutists in 1944. Other simple memorial tablets are located elsewhere, at various sites where other nationals had been incarcerated.

Approximately one mile from the original camp site, on the edge of the escarpment overlooking Weimar, the woodlands have been cleared, and a most impressive and imposing bell tower memorial has been set up to commemorate the fate of the thousands of former inmates of the camp during its eight years of infamy. Three immense circular massed grave sites, each contained within high walls, display very explicit wall murals depicting daily scenes within the camp routine, and linked by an impressive 'Road of Nations', along which have been set up eighteen huge solid stone pylons, with oil flames burning on the tops. Each pylon is dedicated to one of the many nations who had their nationals incarcerated within the camp, and whose country was occupied by the Germans—thus there is not one for the United Kingdom.

Once a year, on the anniversary date of the liberation of the camp, the whole area comes alive with thousands of visitors from all countries, making their pilgrimage to this national centre, carrying their national flags and wreaths to lay on their pylons.

The day went very quickly, and before departing we were given various original booklets and mementoes to associate our visit with the past. We were also given a warm invitation to return the following springtime to attend the fortieth anniversary of the self-liberation of the camp, which was to be a special effort to gather as many original surviving inmates as possible, as it was appreciated that age was critical and many wouldn't be alive for the fiftieth anniversary.

After our return to England, the Royal Air Force Museum at Hendon requested that I prepare a special commemorative cover associated with the involvement of the small party of RAF who were imprisoned in the camp during 1944, to be taken back and cancelled on the 11th April 1985 at the fortieth anniversary celebrations. Accordingly, on the 9th April 1985, my wife and I set off laden with six boxes of covers, all stamped ready for overfranking, a very large boxed poppy wreath, and of course our own luggage. We crossed over the Channel to Paris, taking the overnight express to Frankfurt where we changed trains, joining an East German train for the remainder of the journey. Once again we received a warm welcome at the hotel, though this time we had to stay in Erfurt, about ten miles the other side of the camp, as Weimar was packed full with overseas visitors long since booked in for the occasion.

At Weimar the postal authorities went to considerable care to individually hand cancel each stamped cover, whilst another endorsement was put on with the Buchenwald camp identification. At Buchenwald, the long-awaited three-day celebrations were somewhat harrowing— we were the sole British visitors in the midst of ten thousand others, many of them frail old former inmates, proudly displaying their ragged coloured triangles and their tattered camp registration numbers on their chests. We laid our poppy wreath with quiet dignity on the SOE memorial tablet, providing a great source of interest to the very many visitors who made their way down the roadway from the bunker block, past the crematorium to the new museum in the former Effekten-kammer. It was very moving, my wife and I being embraced by complete strangers, making their sincere messages known in a mixture of broken German, Russian, French and English—all so genuine in their sincere greetings and concern for the events of the past. So many people wished to convey their admiration at the conduct of the brave 'parachutists' who had gone to their fate with such dignity.

Everywhere, we met genuine regret for events that had brought us, as Englishmen, into the camp, and for the events we witnessed with shame to their nation. We met no hostility, and no attempt was made at any time to embarrass us with anti-Western propaganda. The local police were very helpful; with so many vehicles bringing visitors to the camp from hundreds of miles around, the area within four miles of the camp was completely sealed off. We had a hired East German car, yet when we made our identities known, we were given special escorted clearance through each road check, and allocated a special parking lot, right outside the headquarters building itself. Had we been the British Ambassador, we couldn't have received more respectful treatment.

I feel these events of the past must be recorded—I feel guilty that I haven't done more in some ways to do my share. However, I feel that I have done my duty in other ways. The modest little SOE memorial tablet is now recognised by the government departments concerned, and is being improved. Our British Military Mission makes its annual visit on St George's Day, with the full cooperation of the local Soviet military authorities, and the Union Jack now flies, after all these years, over the camp and in the Avenue of the Nations. The RAF commemorative cover was a success—the world now knows about the little band of young, perhaps a little apprehensive, but brave aircrew.

EPILOGUE

The Final Victory

In 1963 Britain announced it had reached agreement over the claims of its servicemen who were, according to International Law, held illegally in Nazi concentration camps, and claimed compensation on their behalf from the West German government. As a result, reparation was made to British servicemen in 1965, but when Australian servicemen lodged their claims they met with a firm rebuttal. The West German government would not investigate their claims for compensation, they declared, until a Peace Treaty to end the war—a war which finished in 1945—had been signed between East and West Germany.

Worse still, when the Australians appealed to their own federal government leaders, they were told their claims could not be proved. Until recently, the Australian and New Zealand governments have consistently denied that any of their servicemen were ever held in concentration camps, and refused to investigate the claims made by a mere handful of men. The same applied in Canada.

While the passing years have not diluted the memories of what these men witnessed and experienced, their protracted pleas for some form of recognition and just compensation were totally rejected or ignored by a succession of chronically slow and indifferent governments. In the more extreme cases, this failure to act caused a tragic alienation of their former servicemen, who felt betrayed by their own political leaders. They had donned their country's uniform and left their homes to fight in a world war, and yet they were being told there was no evidence of their having being held in Buchenwald and other death camps. The author would suggest this evidence has always been easily obtainable, and in most instances is a matter of public record. No one, it seems, gave a damn about the men's claims.

Finally, in light of irrefutable evidence that these servicemen were indeed in such camps, the federal Labor governments of both Australia and New Zealand were stirred into belated action. However, the pressure on them had to be maintained, as they remained strong on perorations and light on results. In the process of researching this book, the ongoing plight of the Australian servicemen was described to me by a disappointed and frustrated former KLB airman, Ray Perry.

During a visit to the United Kingdom in 1963, considerable publicity appeared in the press concerning proposed compensation for people who had suffered Nazi persecution during the world war. I wrote to the office of the High Commissioner for Australia regarding compensation and, following a reply, wrote to the British Foreign Office, who advised that they were looking into the matter with the Federal Republic of Germany, but that Australians would not be covered.

On my return to Western Australia in 1965 I took up this matter with the Australian government, who were not interested and obviously didn't want to know me. I gave up following replies to my letters. In October 1979 there was a report in the newspaper of other Australian servicemen who were illegally interned during the war, in Theresienstadt concentration camp. So I wrote to Dr Klugman, MHR, who had raised the matter in parliament, asking him if he was aware of RAAF men having spent time in Buchenwald concentration camp. He was not aware of this and pursued matters further in parliament, but with little success. Dr Klugman's speeches did, however, attract the attention of Paul Rea of the *Newcastle Herald*, who wrote up my story.

I again took up the matter with the Australian Government through my local member, but again met with all sorts of excuses being brought forward. I had to obtain proof from the International Red Cross in Switzerland, which was time-consuming, and then I was asked to provide the names of all the Australians and New Zealanders who were illegally interned in Buchenwald, together with their present addresses. I would have thought the government, if they had wanted to, would have been in a better position to do this, and felt that had I achieved success, another obstacle would have been put forward...

In March 1983 the Department of Foreign Affairs replied that 'While servicemen interned in concentration camps do have claims in International Law, these claims cannot be settled in the absence of a peace treaty with Germany'. The English servicemen, although Britain does not have a peace treaty either, did receive compensation for their illegal internment.

Over a period of nine years, unrelenting pressure was applied on the Federal governments by journalist Paul Rea, whose dedication to the plight of the Australian servicemen held in Theresienstadt culminated in a moving television documentary, *Where Death Wears a Smile*. A significant breakthrough came when a more compassionate Minister for Foreign Affairs, Bill Hayden, set up a special committee to investigate the claims of the servicemen from Theresienstadt and Buchenwald, in conjunction with the New Zealand government. In February 1986 Senator Sibraa raised the question of compensation in parliament with then Minister for Veterans' Affairs, Senator Gietzelt. His response, which follows, was the first clear indication that a claim for compensation was being pursued.

It is true that an endeavour has been made by Australian ex-servicemen who were placed in Nazi concentration camps in Germany and Czechoslovakia during World War Two to seek some form of reparations or compensation from the West German government. It was not until 1982 that the previous government, the Liberal-National Party government, decided to make representations to the West German government in respect of these matters and it received no assurances that compensation would be paid.

However, since the change of government in 1983, Mr Hayden and I have had several discussions with respect to this matter and an interdepartmental committee has been established under the chairmanship of the Department of Foreign Affairs with representatives from other interested parties, such as the Department of the Prime Minister and Cabinet, the Department of Finance and the Department of the Treasury, for example, as well as the Department of Veterans' Affairs. We recognise that there is a substantial case for some form of compensation for the dwindling number of ex-prisoners of war who were placed in concentration camps because they were considered too unreliable by the Nazis for ordinary POW camps. Their unreliability by Nazi standards was determined by their attempts to escape and to organise against the Nazi regime.

There is no question that some equity should be available to Australian ex-servicemen. The government believes that there is a prima facie case

171

for some form of compensation. The difficulty is that the West German government is not sympathetic to the proposals. Constant endeavours are being made to try to shift the West German government in this respect. All I can tell Senator Sibraa is that the government is determined to press on with the matter. We are not prepared to accept the negative attitude that is being taken by the West German government. We are hopeful that some progress will be made, even if finally it has to come down to some form of ex gratia payment to the dwindling number of Australian prisoners of war. As Senator Sibraa suggests, the film *Where Death Wears a Smile* shows the degree of persecution, torture and other inhuman activities that were carried out in the concentration camps. We believe that there is a very genuine case for the West German government's accepting some responsibility for reparation in these matters.

It was a time of waiting, and the only assurances coming from Canberra were those suggesting patience. The author meantime had supplied the Minister for Veterans' Affairs with a current address list of the eight surviving KLB airmen, having successfully tracked them down all over Australia. It took some time, but as Ray Perry had surmised, any government instrumentality with the incentive to trace these men could have done so with relative ease. Additionally, copies of certain documents which gave irrefutable proof that the men had indeed been in Buchenwald were passed on to the Minister. For their part, the men ensured Canberra remained aware that they were waiting in the wings, by repeatedly pressing their local MPs to check on the progress of their claims, and by writing to the Minister for Veterans' Affairs.

Then, in a policy speech for the upcoming federal election in 1987, Prime Minister Bob Hawke stated that a compensation sum would be paid to Australian ex-servicemen held 'in Nazi concentration camps or like institutions'.

In February 1988 it was all over. The claimants from Buchenwald and Theresienstadt concentration camps, and others such as Auschwitz and Dachau, each received an ex gratia payment of $10 000. The New Zealand government followed suit, and similar compensation payments were made.

In total, 27 payments were made to Australian ex-servicemen; seventeen to former soldiers and ten to former airmen. Peter Thorp, Secretary of the Concentration Camp Committee, revealed to the author that these Australians had been held in the following camps:

AUSCHWITZ: Seven (of whom two were held in auxiliary work camps, and one who for a period had been held at Belsen)
DACHAU: Two
BUCHENWALD: Eight
THERESIENSTADT: Six
LUBLIN: One
STUTTHOFF: One (who was held in an auxiliary work camp)
FLOSSENBURG: Two (both held in an auxiliary work camp)

For most, it was a huge relief after years of denial and rebuttal, but the years of empty words and false promises are not easily forgotten.

* * *

On the weekend of 24/25 June 1988, six of the eight surviving KLB Australians and their wives met in Canberra for a long overdue reunion, and to celebrate their compensation payouts. For Tom Malcolm and Kevin Light in particular it was an opportunity to meet colleagues they had not seen for 40 years, while for Elaine Fairclough it was a chance to talk at last with the men who had shared the events of Buchenwald with her husband. Due to unavoidable circumstances Ray Perry and Les Whellum had been unable to make the trip, but Bob 'Lofty' Mills and his crew members from Buchenwald were all there; he and Jim Gwilliam, Keith Mills and Eric Johnston had stayed in touch over the years and seemed to almost enjoy the novelty of the media interest in their story. It would be the last get-together for the crew; within months Bob Mills had died as the result of a car accident.

Prior to a dinner at the National Press Club, Major-General Alan Morrison, representing the newly incumbent Minister for Veterans' Affairs, Ben Humphreys, formally welcomed the group to Canberra and took them carefully and succinctly through the history of the compensation story. Later, over dinner, Bob Mills eloquently proposed the toast: to absent friends. Elaine Fairclough silently shed a tear.

Suddenly it seemed everyone wanted to know the story from these elderly survivors of Hitler's Holocaust. The press, radio and television people badgered them over the weekend for interviews—all graciously given.

As the weekend wound down late on the Sunday afternoon, and having made my farewells to the others, I stood outside the High Court building with Jim and Pam Gwilliam, reflecting on a weekend of triumph for the KLB group.

'Well, I guess your book has its ending now,' Jim declared as we watched the other men and their wives saying goodbye to each other. 'You know, it's funny how these things turn out. I'd already accepted the fact that nobody cared, and that any thought of compensation was just a bloody pipe dream. Of course it's nice to get the money after all this time, although it wouldn't buy much more these days than a second-hand car and a packet of smokes, but it was nice to have someone go in to bat for us. And seeing these blokes again—crikey, that's made it all worth while. Forty years—it's been a long time!'

We shook hands, Jim took Pam's arm, and they strolled away together as I opened my car door. Pausing for a few moments to look back at the cluster of KLB men and their wives, I felt mixed emotions of sadness and pleasure. They had finally won their long battle for recognition and compensation, but the motive for their reunion had its origins half a world away, in the bloodied dust of a despised place in Germany, and in the inhuman excesses of their captors. Apart from their experiences as wartime aircrew, Buchenwald was their common bond, yet it was quite noticeable that talk amongst them of Hitler's hell camp, set amid Goethe's beloved beech trees, had little place in their weekend of celebration and remembrance.

There are those today who would admonish us to disregard the more horrifying aspects of wartime history, and others whose emphasis is on trivialising such events, but the memories should remain strong, and we should never forget the barbarisms perpetrated in the name of war. During my research for this book I happened across some appropriate words penned by Samuel Taylor Coleridge, and they came back to me as the Buchenwald airmen drifted off on their separate paths once again:

If men could learn from history, what lessons it might teach us! But passion and party blind our eyes, and the light which experience gives us is a lantern on the stern, which shines only on the waves behind us.

I settled into my car, started the engine and engaged low gear, then crunched across the gravel of the car park onto the roadway. Pensively I drove off, as a blood red sun slowly slipped below the Canberra hills.

Appendix

These two poems by KLB airmen were penned on either side of the Buchenwald experience. In the first, Canadian Willie Waldrum presents some emotional post-war reminisces, while Texan Levitt Beck, who died at the camp, seems to sadly prophesy his own tragic and lonely death in a poem he wrote prior to captivity.

KLB (Konzentrationlager Buchenwald): A Reflection

I'll think of you dear KLB.
Again some future day,
When the world is gay and free
And I am so far away.

Of those long appells in pouring rain
With neither boots nor shoes,
And the SS guards who counted us
Hitting whom they choose.

When I bounce my children on my knee
I'll think of those Gypsy kids
Who, instead of wearing ball and chain,
Should have been wearing bibs.

When I lay in my cosy bed at night
I'll think of your hard boards,
With a single blanket to cover us,
And fleas and lice in hordes.

Ironically, I'll think of how
You took our dog-tags from us,
'Nix soldat—civil!' you said,
Smiling fanatically at us.

Yes, you gave us soup and enough black bread
To etch out a mere existence,
Enough to keep us wanting more
And weaken our resistance.

How two of our number lost their lives
For lack of medical aid;
You wouldn't even give them food
To help save them from the grave.

And then: after eight weeks spent in your filthy soul,
Which seemed to me like years,
The Luftwaffe came, took us away,
I felt like shedding tears.

And so to all you Konzentrators,
A toast I offer thee;
Here's wishing you a happy life,
And to Hell with KLB!

Willie Waldrum
Ex-RAF, Ex-KLB

I See it Now

(Written in 1940)

I watched the day turn into nite,
Creeping shadows reached the sky;
Birds flew to their nests,
Still singing as they went;
All mankind lay at rest,
As though heaven sent.
Quiet ne'er before was like this—
Even wind hung softly about the trees,
As if afraid of waking birds,
Sleeping in their nests;
'Twas like another world to me,
And I found myself wishing—
Wishing it were true.

I've suffered—and have hated it,
But in my mind a thought was born,
Making a new path for me—
On which I now find my way.

I see it now—
While I suffer here
I must not question of it;
It is the way of life—
Too much happiness would spoil me;
I'd grown too fond of life on earth
And the after life I seek
Would not be sweet—
We must have our troubles here;
—Our hearts torn by loss
—Our hands made bloody by war
—Our future left unknown.

Levitt C. Beck, Jr
Born: Houston, Texas, 2 January 1920
Died: Buchenwald, Germany, 29 November 1944

The Airmen in Buchenwald

CANADA:

Atkin H.	Grenon L.T.	King M.A.	Sonshine J.R.
Bastable H.	Guilfoyle M.	Kinnis A.G.	Stewart J.A.
Carter-Edwards E.	Harvie J.D.	Leslie D.E.	Waldrum W.A.
Clark D.	Head L.F.	McClenaghan R.	Watson E.C.
Compton G.A.E.	Hetherington S.	Prudham J.E.	Willis C.E.
Crawford J.	High D.	Scullion P.	
Fulsher F.H.	Hodgson T.R.	Shepherd E.G.	
Gibson W.R.	Hoffman C.R.	Smith J.A.	

AUSTRALIA:

Fairclough M.J.	Light K.W.	Mills R.N.
Gwilliam J.P.	Malcolm T.A.	Perry R.W.
Johnston E.L.	Mills K.C.	Whellum L.K.

NEW ZEALAND:

Cullen M.F.	Lamason P.J.

UNITED KINGDOM:

Angus J.W.	Eagle A.D.	Lucas L.J.	Rowe A.
Barnham L.D.	Fernandez J.J.	Marshall W.	Salt F.
Baxter S.	Gould T.	MacPherson A.J.	Sharrate W.S.
Bennett G.	Harper R.	Measures D.K.	Spierenburg S.A.
Blackham T.H.	Heggarty P.W.	Mutter M.E.S.	Taylor P.G.
Booker S.A.	Hemmens P.D.	Nuttall C.W.	Taylor R.J.
Bryden R.	Hughes R.R.	Osselton J.N.	Vinecombe F.
Chapman K.W.	Jackson E.	Percy D.C.	Ward J.D.
Chinn A.J.	Jordin D.F.	Peterson F.	Watmough G.F.
Clark J.	Joyce R.W.	Phelps E.K.	Wesley L.
Davis E.J.	Kay W.	Reid J.D.	Williams L.
Dowdeswell P.	Leverington R.L.	Robb I.A.	

UNITED STATES:

Alexander W.	Edge W.L.	Masters L.O.	Scott G.W.
Allen R.W.	Fix E.E.	Mauk W.E.	Shearer D.R.
Appleman S.M.	Fore J.W.	Mikel G.	Smith J.H.
Bauder W.F.	Freeman E.C.	Mitchell G.E.	Straulka P.
Beck L.C.	Friel E.J.	Moser J.	Suddock D.E.
Bedford R.L.	Granberry W.L.	Pasha A.	Sypher L.H.
Bowen C.E.	Hanson J.T.	Paxton S.K.	Thompson W.H.
Bozarth J.W.	Hastin J.D.	Pecus S.	Vallee E.
Brown R.H.	Heimerman L.A.	Pederson J.W.	Vance I.E.
Carr F.W.	Hilding R.D.	Peletier A.J.	Vincent E.H.
Chalot J.A.	Hoffman R.B.	Pennell S.	Vratny F.
Chapman P.	Horrigan R.J.	Petrich M.R.	Ward R.
Chesshir D.M.	Horwege G.L.	Phelps B.F.	Watson J.P.
Coates B.A.	Hunter H.F.	Powell W.	Williams W.J.
Coffman J.D.	Johnson R.T.	Reynolds I.J.	Wilson P.J.
Cowan F.K.	Larson M.E.	Richey G.	Wojnick R.J.
Crouch M.E.	Little B.	Ritter E.	Zander A.E.
Dauteul D.F.	Ludwig E.F.	Robertson C.W.	Zeiser J.
Dearey R.W.	MacLenahan J.H.	Ryherd W.H.	
Denaro J.D.	McLaughlin D.G.	Salo L.H.	
Duncan J.H.	Martini F.	Scharf B.T.	

Select Bibliography

Beck, Levitt C., *Fighter Pilot*, Wetzel Publishing, 1946

Blackham, Thomas, 'I Survived Buchenwald', *Flying Review*, May 1954

Burney, Christopher, *The Dungeon Democracy*, William Heinemann, 1983

Dencocks, G., (ed.), *In Enemy Hands*, Hurtig Publications, 1983

Foot, M.R.D., *S.O.E. France*, HMSO, 1966

Kogon, Eugen, *The Theory and Practice of Hell*, Farrar, Straus & Cudahy, 1950

Marshall, Bruce, *The White Rabbit*, Evans Bros, 1952

Neave, Airey, *Saturday at M.I.9*, Hodder and Stoughton, 1969

Poller, Walter, *Butchers of Buchenwald*, Souvenir Press, 1961

Strachan, Anthony (ed.), *In the Clutch of Circumstance*, Cappis Press, 1985

Index